CAMBRIDGE LIBRARY COLLECTION

Books of enduring scholarly value

Travel, Middle East and Asia Minor

This collection of travel narratives, primarily from the nineteenth century, describing the topography, antiquities and inhabitants of the Middle East, from Turkey, Kurdistan and Persia to Mesopotamia, Syria, Jerusalem, Sinai, Egypt and Arabia. While some travellers came to study Christian sites and manuscripts, others were fascinated by Islamic culture and still others by the remains of ancient civilizations. Among the authors are several daring female explorers.

Adventures of Baron Wenceslas Wratislaw of Mitrowitz

Of Czech ancestry, Albert Henry Wratislaw (1821–92) was educated at Rugby and Cambridge, and later became a prominent English public-school headmaster. At Cambridge he became interested in the literature and history of Bohemia and in 1849 he travelled there for the first time, quickly becoming proficient in the language. Upon his return home he began a lifetime of immersion in Czech literature. Published in 1862, this book was the first translation into English of a major Czech prose work. It is the vivid true story of a Bohemian nobleman's journey to, imprisonment in, and return from Constantinople in the late sixteenth century. Wratislaw's translation and brief introduction to Bohemian history proved popular and helped bring Czech literature and history to a wider audience.

Cambridge University Press has long been a pioneer in the reissuing of out-of-print titles from its own backlist, producing digital reprints of books that are still sought after by scholars and students but could not be reprinted economically using traditional technology. The Cambridge Library Collection extends this activity to a wider range of books which are still of importance to researchers and professionals, either for the source material they contain, or as landmarks in the history of their academic discipline.

Drawing from the world-renowned collections in the Cambridge University Library and other partner libraries, and guided by the advice of experts in each subject area, Cambridge University Press is using state-of-the-art scanning machines in its own Printing House to capture the content of each book selected for inclusion. The files are processed to give a consistently clear, crisp image, and the books finished to the high quality standard for which the Press is recognised around the world. The latest print-on-demand technology ensures that the books will remain available indefinitely, and that orders for single or multiple copies can quickly be supplied.

The Cambridge Library Collection brings back to life books of enduring scholarly value (including out-of-copyright works originally issued by other publishers) across a wide range of disciplines in the humanities and social sciences and in science and technology.

Adventures of Baron Wenceslas Wratislaw of Mitrowitz

TRANSLATED BY
ALBERT HENRY WRATISLAW

CAMBRIDGE UNIVERSITY PRESS

Cambridge, New York, Melbourne, Madrid, Cape Town,
Singapore, São Paolo, Delhi, Mexico City

Published in the United States of America by Cambridge University Press, New York

www.cambridge.org
Information on this title: www.cambridge.org/9781108052016

© in this compilation Cambridge University Press 2013

This edition first published 1862
This digitally printed version 2013

ISBN 978-1-108-05201-6 Paperback

ADVENTURES OF BARON WENCESLAS WRATISLAW.

ADVENTURES OF

BARON WENCESLAS WRATISLAW

OF MITROWITZ.

WHAT HE SAW IN THE TURKISH METROPOLIS, CONSTANTINOPLE;

EXPERIENCED IN HIS CAPTIVITY; AND AFTER HIS

HAPPY RETURN TO HIS COUNTRY,

COMMITTED TO WRITING IN THE YEAR OF

OUR LORD 1599.

LITERALLY TRANSLATED FROM THE ORIGINAL BOHEMIAN

By A. H. WRATISLAW, M.A.

HEAD-MASTER OF THE GRAMMAR SCHOOL, BURY ST. EDMUNDS,
AND FORMERLY FELLOW AND TUTOR OF CHRIST'S
COLLEGE, CAMBRIDGE.

LONDON:

BELL AND DALDY, 186, FLEET STREET.

1862.

CONTENTS.

INTRODUCTION.

HE work to which I have come forward to ask the attention of the British public was written as long ago as 1599, and was then intended, apparently, only for private circulation. It was written in the Bohemian or Czesko-Slavonic language, by one who was perfect master of it, and the book itself is described by Jungmann, in his *Historie Literatury Czeské*, in the following words :— "The author relates his journey, and much about the manners and customs of the Turks in a natural, vigorous, pure, and manly style." It remained in manuscript till 1777, when it was published by Pelzel at Prague, and a second edition was published by Kramerius in 1807. I have made my translation from the latter edition, and it will be found to differ very widely from the German translation of 1786, in which the translator, for instance, introduces a violent tirade against the celibacy of the clergy, not one word of which is in the printed Bohemian edition, which I possess ; omits the pathetic and deeply pious peroration of the whole ; and actually makes Mount Olivet, instead of Mount Olympus, visible from Constantinople. The work is divided into four books, the first of which treats of the journey to, the second the residence at, Constantinople, the third gives an account of the captivity of the author and his companions, and the fourth of their deliverance and return. It is rarely that a mere boy has gone through so much for the sake of his religion, and still more rarely does it occur that so great a sufferer is able to give so clear and graphic an account of his own misfortunes, and those of others. The first book appears to have been taken from a journal actually sent home to the writer's family, and afterwards interspersed with anecdotes and digressions on Turkish life and manners; the rest were manifestly written from a very vivid, and often very painful, recollection of the scenes which they describe. It will, perhaps, be some additional recommendation to Baron Wratislaw's work to mention, at the outset, that the ambassadors of Queen Elizabeth of England, and Henry IV. of France, whose names I find, from Von Hammer, to have been respectively Edward Burton, and M. de Brèves, took a prominent part in the liberation of the captives; and that it was to the Christian friendship of the former that they were indebted for their eventual escape through Hungary. An account of the embassy was also written in German by the apothecary, Frederic Seidel, but I have been unable to obtain a copy of it.

The Czesko-Slavonic or Bohemian language is spoken by the race inhabiting Bohemia watered by the Elbe, or *Labe,* and the Moldau, or *Veltava;* Moravia, watered by the March, or *Morava;* and Slovakia, or the district of the Slovaks, in the north of Hungary. It is altogether spoken by about eight millions of people. It differs from the Polish in not having retained the nasal sounds of *a* and *e,* which connect the objective case feminine, in Polish, with the *am* and *em* of the Latin accusative. In Polish, also, the accent falls almost invariably on the penultimate; in Bohemian on the first syllable of every word. Bohemian is connected with Greek by possessing prosodiacal quantity, *i. e.* long and short vowels, independently of accent—a peculiarity which has been lost by every Slavonic dialect except the Servian, and in that it is said to be far less distinct than in the Bohemian. All the Slavonic dialects agree in retaining the *locative* case, which appears occasionally in Greek, and in Latin is found only in the names of places, and in some few other words, as *humi, domi, ruri.* They also agree in a use of the instrumental case almost exactly corresponding to that which is commonly called the *dativus propositi,* but which would be far more properly designated the *idiomatic dative of the predicate* in Latin, being simply an occasional artifice to distinguish the predicate from the subject, when both are substantives, in the absence of an article, of which the uncorrupted Slavonic dialects are equally destitute with the Latin and early Greek.

The early history of Bohemia is very mythological, and has been well treated, for the first time, in a philosophical spirit, by the historian Francis Palacky. During great part of the ninth century Moravia was the seat of government of a powerful kingdom, whose prince, Moymir, became a Christian. In 844 fourteen Bohemian *Lechs,* or lords, determined to embrace Christianity, betook themselves to King Louis the German at Ratisbon, and were solemnly baptized on the 1st of January, 845. But the principal glory of the conversion of the Slavonians belongs to Cyrillus and Methodius, the sons of the patrician Leo of Thessalonica, a town then inhabited by a half Greek, half Slavonic population. Rastislaw of Moravia heard of the conversion of the Bulgarian monarch, Boris, by the younger of the two brothers, Methodius, and sent, in 862, an embassy to the Emperor Michael of Constantinople to request the presence of Slavonic Christian teachers, as the German priests were unable to instruct his people in their own language. Cyrillus and Methodius came themselves in answer to this petition. After four years and a-half of activity in Moravia, the brothers visited, and were well received by, Pope Adrian II. at Rome. Cyrillus, the inventor of the so-called Cyrillic alphabet, on which the modern Russian is founded, died at Rome in 868, but his brother Methodius was appointed by the Pope to the dignity of archbishop in Moravia and Pannonia.

In 871 the Duke of Bohemia, Borzivoy, and his wife Ludmilla, the latter of whom has a statue and chapel, as a saint, in the cathedral at Prague, were baptized. The Slavonic and Latin liturgies appear to have both been in use in Bohemia from the earliest times. Borzivoy was succeeded by Spitihnew I, and he by his brother Wratislaw I, whose wife, Drahomira, could never be converted to Christianity. After the death of Wratislaw, Drahomira had her mother-in-law, Ludmilla, murdered, and excited her younger son, Boleslaw, to murder his Christian brother Wenceslaw in 936. Boleslaw the Cruel was a successful ruler and warrior, and left the crown to his son, Boleslaw II, surnamed the Pious, in whose reign the first monasteries were founded in Bohemia (967-999). Under the sons of Boleslaw II, Bohemia was conquered by Boleslaw the Brave, of Poland, who was afterwards expelled, and the old native dynasty of the Przemyslides replaced on the throne. The power of Bohemia was restored by Bretislaw I, who was followed by Spitihnew II, whose brother and successor, Wratislaw II, obtained a royal crown from the Emperor Henry IV. and the Pope in 1086. Under Wratislaw's successor, Bretislaw II, the Slavonic ritual, which had long been upheld by popular favour against the efforts of Rome, appears to have become confined to a single monastery, and to have been at length absolutely forbidden by Pope Gregory VII. in 1094; but the Slavonic monks were not ejected from their monastery on the Sazava till 1096. The history from that time to 1197 is comparatively uninteresting, and the only thing to remark in it is the increase of power obtained by the bishops and clergy, and their constant interference in state affairs.

With Przemysl Ottakar I. matters took a decisive turn, and Bohemia became, and continued for several centuries, a powerful and independent kingdom. Under this king and his successor, Wenzel I, new orders of monks and nuns were introduced into the country. But Bohemia's greatest splendour was reached under the next king, Przemysl Otta-kar II, who ruled from the Riesengebirge in the north to the Adriatic in the south, and whose protection was sought not merely by many dukes in Poland and Silesia, but even by Verona, Friuli, and many other important Italian towns. But it was the fate of Ottakar to be encompassed by trea-cherous friends, and he was finally defeated and killed by the Emperor Rudolf of Hapsburg in 1278. Wenzel II. suc-ceeded to a kingdom greatly reduced in power, and with Wenzel III. the ancient dynasty of the Przemyslides ended in 1306.

During the preceding century the people had been gradu-ally forming themselves into regular hereditary classes, which were now legally recognized. Great intestine troubles were finally healed by the marriage of the Bohemian Princess Elizabeth with John, the only son of the King of the Ro-mans, Henry VII. of Luxemburg, in 1310. Till 1333, King John ruled alone, when he associated with him his son Charles, under the title of Margrave of Moravia. In 1340, King John became blind, and, in 1346, he fell at Creçy, repulsing the entreaties of his barons that he would leave the hopeless field with the memorable words:—" Tot bohdá nebude, by kral Czesky z boje utiekal;" " Please God it will never come to pass that a king of Bohemia flees out of battle." He was succeeded by his son Charles, who founded the University of Prague in 1348, and was crowned Emperor at Rome, in 1355, by the title of Charles IV. Both the Emperor and the Pope, Gregory XI, died in the same year, 1378.

Wenzel IV. succeeded both as King of Bohemia and King of the Romans, but was deposed from the latter dignity in 1400. It was during his reign that the great schism in the Roman Church occurred, and that the intellectual movement began in Bohemia, which resulted in the great Hussite wars. Conrad Waldhauser, Milicz of Kremsier, and Mathias of Janow, caused a great deal of religious enthusiasm by preaching and writing. And the University of Prague had become so famous that there is reason to believe it contained, in 1408, no less than 200 doctors and masters, 500 bachelors, and above 30,000 students, all divided into four nations,—the Bohemian, Bavarian, Saxon, and Polish. Doctors and masters might lecture as they pleased, but bachelors were obliged to make use of the works of some known master of the universities of Prague, Paris, or Oxford. Thus some of Wycliffe's works became known at Prague even in his lifetime, and after the marriage of the Bohemian Princess Anne with Richard II. of England, in 1381, the intercourse between the two countries became very close and active, and several influential Bohemian doctors more or less adopted and defended the views of the great Englishman.

But the leading spirits of those to whom the principles of Wycliffe became more than mere matters of speculative dis-

cussion were JOHN HUS and JEROME of Prague. John
Hus was born, in 1369, in the village of Husinetz, of ple-
beian parents in comparatively easy circumstances. He took
the degree of Bachelor of Arts at Prague in September, 1393,
that of Bachelor of Divinity in 1394, and, finally, that of
Master of Arts in January, 1396. In 1398 he appeared as a
public teacher in the university, and, in 1399, came to an
open rupture with his colleagues in a disputation held at the
parsonage of St. Michael, in the old town of Prague, through
defending some of the principles of Wycliffe. He was,
nevertheless, elected Dean of the Faculty of Philosophy on
Oct. 16, 1401, and presented to the Preachership at the
Bethlehem Chapel at Prague. In October, 1402, he obtained
the highest academic dignity, the Rectorship of the University, which he held to the end of April, 1403.

J erome of Prague was a member of a family belonging to
the inferior order of nobility, and was several years younger
than Hus, with whom he early contracted an intimate friendship. More vivacious and less steadfast than his grave and
stable friend, he wandered through Europe as a student, and
brought from Oxford several of Wycliffe's works, which
had been previously unknown in Bohemia. He took the
degree of Bachelor of Arts in Sept. 1498, obtained a dispen-
sation from the duty of teaching in schools for two years,
visited the universities of Cologne and Heidelberg, and took
the degree of Master of Arts at the University of Paris. He
appears to have taken an *ad eundem* degree at Prague in
1407. He visited Palestine and Jerusalem, and was, according to his own statement, at the latter place when the first
condemnation of Wycliffe's principles took place at Prague
in 1403, in which twenty-one articles alleged to be taken out
of Wycliffe's works were condemned, in addition to the
twenty-four condemned in the Council of London, in 1382.

Of the four nations of which the University of Prague was composed, followers of Wycliffe were found only among the Bohemians. Indeed, as each separate nation possessed a vote, the Bohemians were regularly outvoted by the Germans in the university, the Polish nation having since the foundation of the University of Cracow consisted almost entirely of German Silesians, Pomeranians, and Prussians. An appeal upon university affairs was made to King Wenzel, who spoke with the greatest severity to Hus, who soon afterwards was seized with so serious an illness that his life was despaired of. But soon, through the influence of Nicholas of Lobkovitz, supported by the representatives of the King of France, and the University of Paris, King Wenzel, finding that the three votes of the foreigners rested on no statute, but only on custom, issued an edict, (Jan. 18, 1409,) that from thenceforth the Bohemian nation should have three votes, and the foreigners only one. The final result was that the German professors and students almost entirely left Prague, and the numbers of those who quitted the university must have been very large, from the fact that no less than *two thousand* were counted departing in a single day.

In 1409 the singular spectacle of three rival Popes was exhibited to the Christian world, and in 1410, that of three rival Kings of the Romans. On July 16, 1410, the prelates and clergy solemnly burned the books of Wycliffe at Prague, and on the 18th the archbishop formally excommunicated Hus and his friends. Hus was protected by the court and by a large party in the country, and refused to give up preaching, saying that it was his duty to obey God rather than man. His appeal was rejected, and the proceedings of the archbishop confirmed by Pope John XXIII, and he himself was cited to appear at the Court of Rome to defend himself within a given time. In 1411 the archbishop laid the whole town of Prague under an interdict. King Wenzel felt himself personally aggrieved by these proceedings of the spiritual power, and took violent measures against the archbishop and clergy. Seeing the uselessness of the course he had taken, the archbishop, on July 6, became formally reconciled to both the king and the adherents of Hus, but soon afterwards died.

In 1412, John XXIII. issued bulls proclaiming a crusade against Ladislaw, King of Naples, and promising to all who should take the cross in person, or provide armed substitutes, or contribute money towards the expenses of the war, the same indulgences and remission of sins that had been granted to those who assumed the cross for the liberation of the Holy Sepulchre. The publication of these bulls in Prague caused fresh excitement; Hus and his adherents publicly preached against them, and commented severely on the anti-Christian conduct of the Pope. One of the king's favourites, Woksa of Waldstein, and Jerome of Prague, contrived a satirical procession, in imitation of that which had preceded the burning of Wycliffe's works, and finished by publicly burning the bulls. Three young persons were put to death for contradicting the clergy in different churches, and maintaining that the promised remission was a mere deception. When accused of not giving in his views in writing to the Dean of Theology, Hus replied that he was ready to do so, as soon as his opponents, who accused him of heresy, engaged to prove him a heretic, under pain, in case of failure, of suffering the same penalty, viz. that of being burned as heretics, which they were endeavouring to impose upon him,—an invitation which they declined. In July, 1412, Hus was excommunicated in the most severe and horrible manner; no one, under penalty of the same, was allowed to give him food, drink, or shelter, and the faithful were called upon to arrest and deliver him up ; neither did King Wenzel offer any impediment to the publication of this excommunication.

The king appointed a commission for the purpose of healing the breaches in the national church, and was so offended by the conduct of the papal party that he deposed and banished the four theological professors of the university. Hus, during these proceedings, spent most of his time in a castle built on the spot where afterwards rose the town of Tabor. Here he wrote his *Tractatus de Ecclesiâ,* his Bohemian *Postilla,** and many other works, besides carrying on a considerable correspondence with his friends. He also invented the system of Bohemian orthography, which is now almost entirely dominant; but his Latin treatise on the subject has not yet been printed. While in the country, Hus took every opportunity of preaching to the people on market-days and similar occasions, and thus made his exile contribute to the promulgation of his doctrines.

In the beginning of 1413, Pope John XXIII. held a small council at Rome, at which the forty-five articles selected from Wycliffe's works were again condemned by a bull, dated Feb. 2, which was subjected in Bohemia to brief but very biting criticism. This criticism is found in manuscripts under the name of Hus, who, however, always disowned its authorship, and ascribed it to his friend Magister Jesenetz. On Dec. 9, 1413, the bull was issued which appointed a General Council to meet at Constance, on the 1st of Nov. 1414. Sigismund, the brother of King Wenzel, had succeeded the deposed Bohemian monarch as King of the Romans, had been formally reconciled to him, and was now exerting himself in every possible way to forward the great work of the Council. Sigismund entered into direct

* Reflections on the Sunday Epistles and Gospels.

correspondence with Hus, and invited him to appear personally at Constance, promising not only a safe-conduct, but
also every assistance towards bringing matters to a satis-
factory conclusion, and Hus engaged to appear.

On Nov. 28, Hus was arrested at Constance, in spite of
the protest of the Bohemian nobles, to whom his safety had
been entrusted.　King Sigismund at first protested against
the arrest as a violation of his safe-conduct, and was only
with great difficulty induced to acquiesce in it.　In March,
1415, Pope John fled from Constance, and on Palm-Sunday,
March 24, the keys of Hus's prison were given up to King
Sigismund, who, instead of setting him at liberty, placed
him in the hands of the Bishop of Constance, by whom he
was imprisoned in chains at his castle of Gottlieben.　On the
4th of April, Jerome of Prague, in spite of the warnings of
Hus, came to Constance, challenged a trial, and demanded
a safe-conduct.　Finding that proceedings would be immediately taken against him, he fled, but was arrested at Hirschau,
not far from the frontiers of Bohemia, and brought back to
Constance. Hus was heard thrice, with a manifest determination to put him to death, and, in fact, a Bohemian who had,
on the first hearing, got behind the clerk, who read the documents aloud, saw the sentence of condemnation all ready
prepared among the other papers, and it was only prevented
from being read by the urgent remonstrances of the king.
But after the third hearing, on July 8, Sigismund, in a con-
fidential conversation with a number of cardinals and prelates, warned them against placing any confidence either in
Hus or in Jerome, even if they recanted, and urged them
to make an end of the matter as quickly as possible, as he
should himself soon be obliged to leave the council.

Endeavours were made to induce Hus to recant; but he
uniformly refused to do so, unless proofs of his errors were

produced to him out of the *Scriptures,* the decision of which alone he professed himself ready to recognize. But he was never allowed to defend himself, or prove the innocence of any of his doctrines, being simply required to answer yes or no to the questions put to him. On the 6th of July, 260 passages from Wycliffe's works were read aloud and condemned, and then thirty articles taken out of the writings of Hus along with the other evidence and the whole proceedings against him. Not only accusations, which he believed himself to have refuted, were brought against him, but even such absurdities as that he had represented himself to be the fourth person in the Holy Trinity. Sigismund blushed when Hus reminded him that he had come thither voluntarily under the protection of his safe-conduct. Hus was then condemned to be degraded from the priesthood, and delivered over to the secular arm. The sentence was immediately carried into execution, and the ashes of the martyr were gathered together and flung into the Rhine.

Jerome of Prague recanted on Sept. 10, 1415, relapsed again on the opening of a fresh process against him, and was finally condemned and martyred in 1416.

Meanwhile the favourers of Hus were splitting into two parties, that of the inhabitants of Prague—afterwards called the Calixtines, from Pope Calixtus III, negotiations with whom appeared at one time likely to take a favourable turn—whose views originated with learned professors and masters, and in the university, and that which arose from a spontaneous fermentation in the popular mind, which afterwards became known as the sect of the Taborites. The University of Prague took a middle course between the Fathers of Constance and the extreme Hussites; but on March 10, 1417, it spoke decidedly to the effect that, while those who received the communion in only one kind ought

to be borne with, yet the right and original manner of receiving it was under both kinds. Hence the Utraquist
doctrine of the reception of the communion *sub utrâque specie*
took fast root in Bohemia.

In 1419, King Wenzel began at length to take measures
against the Hussites, although his courtiers and enlightened
favourites had always been among the most zealous and re-
solute adherents of the new doctrines. Several of these, in
consequence, left his service; among whom the most remarkable were Nicolas of Pistna, Hus or Husinetz, and the famous
one-eyed JOHN ZISKA of Trotznow. Orthodox priests were
placed in all the benefices; communion in both kinds was
refused to the laity; and many undertook long pilgrimages
in order to meet with clergymen who would not refuse them
the cup. And the Hussite clergy, who were even driven
from their old head-quarters at Austi, encamped in tents
on a broad hill near the river Luznitz, which was surrounded
on three sides by deep ravines full of water, and only connected with the mainland by an isthmus, thus forming a
natural fortress. Here, in the summer of 1419, they held
service in the open air, with the peasantry, who crowded to
them, and named the place, in their almost exclusively Biblical
language, Mount Tabor, a word which also signifies a camp
in Slavonic. On July 22 no less than 42,000 persons
assembled there for devotional purposes, and separated again
with perfect quiet. But on Aug. 16, King Wenzel himself
died, and his legitimate successor was his brother King
Sigismund, under whose auspices the Council of Constance
had been held, and Hus and Jerome condemned to the
flames.

Sigismund was in Hungary at the time, and determined to
postpone his Bohemian affairs to the prosecution of the war
against the Turks, in which he was engaged. The Bohemian

Estates met and required their future king to promise complete religious freedom, free use of the cup in the communion in all churches, prohibition of the publication of papal
bulls before their approval by the royal council, and of all
insults to the memory of Huss and Jerome, and the use of
the Bohemian language in courts of justice. To these things
the town of Prague added a request, that, at the celebration
of the mass, at least the gospel and epistle might be read in
the vulgar tongue. Sigismund simply replied that he intended to carry on the government as his father, Charles IV,
had done before him ; and at Kuttenberg, on May 12, 1420,
drove the deputies of the people of Prague from him with
reproaches, demanding that all their weapons should be
delivered up to him, and they should then see what favour he
would show them. "War to the death !" became then the
universal cry in Prague, and messengers were sent for help
to Tabor, which had just been founded, by the advice of Ziska,
as a fortress of refuge for the Hussites, and to the other allied
towns.

The first crusade against the Hussites now began in earnest.
The Taborites entered Prague, and the host of Sigismund
was entirely routed by the united forces of the Hussites before the walls of Prague, on July 14, 1420. The celebrated
Four Articles of Prague were then drawn up as the public
confession of the nation, to the following effect:—

1. "That the Word of God be published and preached
in the kingdom of Bohemia by Christian priests without let
or hindrance.

2. "That the holy sacrament of the body and blood of
Christ be freely offered under both forms of bread and
wine to all faithful Christians, not incapacitated by deadly
sin.

3. "That worldly possessions be taken from priests and

monks, and that they live henceforth conformably to the Scripture, and to the life of Christ and the Apostles.

4. " That all deadly sins, and especially those of an open nature, be brought to judgment and punished, and that an end be put to the evil and false report of this land."

On Oct. 31 the Crusaders suffered a second defeat while attempting to relieve the garrison of the Vyssegrad, or citadel of Prague, and Ziska led the Taborites to success after success in the south of Bohemia. On Feb. 6, 1421, a junction was effected between the forces of Ziska and those of Prague, the result of which was that Sigismund disbanded his army, and hastened out of Bohemia, which was soon overrun by the Hussites, who then entered Moravia. And on April 21, to the great astonishment of all men, Archbishop Conrad, of Prague, declared his adhesion to the Four Articles. Ziska lost his remaining eye at the siege of the castle of Rabi by an arrowshot, but still continued to act as general with similar success. In fact, this loss caused him to be more dependent on others, and thus spread a greater amount of military skill and science in his army.

Of the second great crusade, in the latter part of 1421, but little is known, except that it exercised great cruelties, besieged Saaz unsuccessfully, and was so disgracefully defeated that the common remark was that the Crusaders entertained so pious a horror of the infidel Hussites that they would not so much as look them in the face. Sigismund afterwards suffered a tremendous defeat at Deutsch-brod on Jan. 8, 1422.

Ziska himself, it must be remarked, was not a genuine Taborite, but headed a party which stood midway between the party of Prague, afterwards called the Calixtines, and the Taborites. This is proved by the fact of the separation of those more particularly attached to the person of " Father

Ziska" from the Taborites, under the name of the "Orphans," after his death.   Indeed, in 1422 a quarrel took place between Ziska and the Taborites, who were never more than partially reconciled, though Ziska resumed the chief command of the army as before. In the same year Prince Sigismund Korybut of Poland was elected Regent of Bohemia, and recognized as such by Ziska.

The third crusade was determined upon at the Diet of Nuremberg, in September and October, 1422, but was ended by an armistice for a year, and the total disbandment of the crusading army in November. In 1423, Ziska carried his victorious arms not only into Moravia, but into Hungary. But 1424 was Ziska's "bloody year," during which, in his hatred of hypocrisy, and of what he supposed to be coquetting with Rome, he injured his own nation as much as the com mon enemy. He died of the plague, commending himself to God, not far from the Moravian frontier, on the 11th of Oct. 1424. His great victories were won through the extraordinary drill and discipline of his infantry and moving fortress of waggons, the celerity of his marches and manœuvres, and his skill in the employment of artillery.

Ziska was succeeded by Prokop the Bald, otherwise called Prokop the Great. Under him the Bohemians assumed the offensive, and victoriously invaded Austria and Silesia. On March 18, 1427, Pope Martin V. appointed Henry, Bishop of Winchester, his cardinal-legate, with most extensive powers, in Bohemia, Hungary, and Germany. A diet was held at Frankfort, and a fourth crusade against the Hussites begun. But on August 2 the whole army which had invaded Bohemia was seized with a panic, and the cardinal, when on his way to join it, met it in full retreat. The diet met again at Frankfort, and on Dec. 3 the Hussite-tax was imposed throughout the German Empire, for the purpose of carrying on the war. Meanwhile the Bohemians were actively and victoriously invading the neighbouring districts of Germany.

Cardinal Julian Cesarini became the new legate in Germany and Bohemia. Martin V. died, and Eugene IV. succeeded to the tiara. Cardinal Julian determined once more to try the fortune of war before entering on negotiations, for the purpose of which the Council of Basel had been summoned, and ought to have been opened on March 3, 1431. Although his presence was required at Basel as President of the Council, he nevertheless entered Bohemia at the head of an army of 40,000 cavalry and 90,000 infantry, which fled in confusion at the mere sound of the waggons and war-hymns of the Bohemians, near Tauss, on Aug. 14, 1431. Thus ended the fifth and last crusade against the Hussites.

The better path of negotiation was at length entered upon by the Council of Basel, and its President, Cardinal Julian, the latter of whom was now fully convinced of the impossibility of success in dealing with the Bohemians by violent measures. Owing to a quarrel in Hungary the Orphans separated from the Taborites, and entered into closer relations with the moderate Utraquists of Prague. It is remarked by Palacky that the Taborites represented the future Calvinists, and the Orphans the Lutherans; while the Calixtines of Prague approximated rather to the Church of England.

Fifteen deputies to the council were chosen by the Bohemians, among whom were their great general, Prokop, and the Taborite-Englishman, Peter Payne, the former of whom formed a singular friendship with the cardinal-president, and the latter took a prominent part in the disputations and discussions at Basel. Prokop, at the conclusion of the arguments, made a remarkable apology for himself and appeal to the council, which is worth extracting. He said that he had noticed that people seemed to imagine that he had killed many human beings with his own hand. He would not, he said, maintain an untruth for the whole world; but this was utterly false, for he had never shed a drop of blood with his own hand, much less slain anybody himself. He had certainly held the chief command in many battles, in which many men had perished; but this was not his fault, but that of the Pope and cardinals, whom he had often called upon to give up wars and temporal matters, and busy themselves with the Church reform that was so much wanted,—the purpose for which the present council was convened. They should neither oppose the free preaching of the Word of God, nor the communion in both kinds, which was held by the Greek Church also; neither should they damn and persecute those who differed from them in opinion, for instance, the Waldenses, who, poor as they were, were yet honourable and respectable people. They should take care that in the multitude of ecclesiastical regulations God's law was not forgotten, and that the reproach made by our Lord to the Jews (Mark vii. 8.) should not hold good with regard to the present church.

The deputies departed with words of kindness and friendship from the cardinal; and as they left the hall in which the meetings had been held, an Italian bishop forced his way to them through the crowd, shook hands with them, and began to weep bitterly.

After two embassies from the council to the Bohemians, the first "Compactata" were settled, which allowed the Bohemians and Moravians the use of the cup in the communion, but reserved the rights of bishops to appoint preachers, and those of the Church to possess property, and appoint clergymen to administer it. Soon afterwards a civil war broke out between the great nobles and the people of Prague on the one side, and the Taborites and the inhabitants

of the smaller towns on the other, which was finally decided,
unfavourably for the latter party, in the battle of Lipan, on
May 30, 1434, which broke for ever the power of the Taborites and Orphans. No quarter was given, and both Prokop
the Great and Prokop the Little were killed. The declara-
tion of Prokop the Great at the Council of Basel renders it
hard to believe the rhetorical account of Æneas Sylvius, that,
when he saw the battle was lost, he gathered round him his
body-guard, composed rather of the strongest men than of
those whom he loved best, rushed into the midst of the enemy
and perished, *non tam victus quam vincendo fessus.*

The great advantage of the battle of Lipan fell to the
Calixtine party, headed by Magister John Rokycana, who
was eventually chosen Utraquist Archbishop of Prague, but
who was never regularly consecrated, as the confirmation of
the election could never be obtained from the Pope. Further
negotiations were carried on, the "Compactata" were solemnly
published, and Sigismund was acknowledged king in July,
1436, but died on Dec. 9, 1437. He was succeeded by
Albert of Austria, who died in 1439. His widowed queen,
Elizabeth, became the mother of a son, Ladislaw Postumus,
who, while still a minor, was elected King of Bohemia,
under the "gubernatorship" of George of Podiebrad, before
whose complete recognition as regent unsuccessful attempts
were made by the Utraquists to effect an union with the
Greek Church. Ladislaw died of the plague in 1457, and
George of Podiebrad was elected king, whose reign was
spent in vain attempts to obtain the confirmation of the "Compactata," and of the election of Rokycana as archbishop, from
the Pope. George of Podiebrad exercised the most extraordinary influence in Europe during his reign, and was generally regarded as the greatest soldier and statesman of his
day. He died on March 22, 1476, almost immediately

after the death of the Utraquist Archbishop Elect, Rokycana.

Two of the most remarkable events of his regency and
reign were the complete suppression of the singular re-
publican community of the Taborites, and the rise of the
Bohemian Brethren.   A curious account of the former,
shortly before their suppression in 1452, is given by an eyewitness, which I abridge from Palacky :—

"Æneas Sylvius Piccolomini, afterwards Pope Pius II,
and his companions, when on their way with a mission from
the Emperor Frederic III. to the Bohemian Parliament at
Beneschau, were overtaken by the approach of night in the
neighbourhood of Tabor.   For fear of robbers and other
roving bands of armed men, they did not think it advisable
to spend the night in a village, but sent on to the town of
Tabor to announce their arrival, and to ask for shelter for
the night.   'We preferred,' says Æneas, 'to entrust ourselves to the wolves rather than to the hares.   At this the
Taborites were delighted, and streamed out in crowds to
meet and salute us.   Extraordinary spectacle !   A rude and
boorish people wishing to appear courteous !   The weather
was rainy and cold.   They came to meet us partly on foot,
partly on horseback ; some in light coats, others in skins ;
one with one eye, another with one hand ; this man without
a saddle, that without boots and spurs ; all without order,
and with plenty of noise, bringing, however, presents of
welcome—fish, wine, and beer.   The town itself stands on a
level projection over declivities and waters, and is surrounded
with a double wall, provided with a good many towers.   On
the side on which it joins the main land it is additionally
protected by a deep ditch and a thick wall. Whoever wishes
to enter here must do so through a threefold gate.   The first
gate has a wall, twenty feet broad and forty feet high, and a

strong tower over it. At the entrance there are two shields to be seen; on the one is painted an angel with the cup, as though inviting people to taste it; on the other is a portrait of the blind old Ziska, formerly the most distinguished leader of the Taborites; for, though they detest the images of saints, yet his image is everywhere held in the greatest honour. There are no regular streets in the town, but where each man first casually pitched his tent, there he afterwards built a house of wood or mud. In the public market-place a number of military engines are placed, to terrify their neighbours. There are about 4,000 men capable of bearing arms in the town; but since they can no longer issue forth as formerly to obtain booty, they have become effeminate, and some maintain themselves by weaving in wool and flax, and others by trade. There are, however, a good many rich people among them, and household furniture is everywhere handsome and even magnificent. Formerly there was no separate property among the Taborites; the booty taken from the enemy was collected and applied by the brethren in common, and one supplied what another wanted. Now, however, each lives for himself; love towards the neighbour has waxed cold; one is in luxury, while another dies of hunger. There stands in the town a wooden house, built something like a village barn, which they call their Temple; there the word is preached, the gospel daily expounded, and the sacrament distributed at a single unconsecrated and unhallowed altar. Their priests wear no tonsure, neither do they shave their beards. The congregation brings to their houses meat and drink, as requisite, and contributes three-score groschen per head, that they may have money for their minor wants. No tithes or money-offerings are brought to the altar. The greatest care is taken that everybody attends the sermon diligently; whoever neglects this is punished.

Nevertheless, they are not all of one creed; in Tabor every-body may believe what he likes.   There are there Nicolai-tans, Arians, Manichæans, Armenians, Nestorians, Beren-garians, and Poor Men of Lyons; but the Waldenses, the mortal foes of the see of Rome, are in especial estimation.'

"Æneas Sylvius stayed in Tabor with a very rich and respected citizen, from whose mouth he obtained the greater part of the above information.   This man also showed his guest a valuable statue of the Virgin Mary and the crucified Redeemer, which he preserved reverentially among his trea-sures, but refused to be persuaded to proclaim in a more open manner his attachment to the Church of Rome.   Never-theless, Æneas Sylvius, on his return from Beneschau, whilst his colleagues remained at table in Tabor, again visited his former host, to whose house the most considerable citizens, priests, and deacons came immediately to salute him. All these spoke Latin, for, as he says, ' this faithless people had this one good quality, that it loved the sciences.'   The conversation soon became a dispute, in which an especial share was taken by Nicholas, whom they called their bishop, ' a man full of evil days;' Wenzel Coranda, ' an old slave of the devil;' and John Galet, who had not long before fled thither for refuge from Poland, where he was to have been burnt.   Æneas, though unwillingly, stood his ground, for fear of giving the Taborites, by his silence, occasion to boast that he, a bishop of the Romish faith, had either not ven-tured or not been able to withstand their arguments.   Of course they parted on the same terms as they had met.   But Æneas thanked God when he was again out of that ' nest of heretics,' that 'synagogue of Satan,' and found himself again in the open air; ' I felt,' said he, ' as though I had escaped from hell.''

I cannot here omit Æneas Sylvius's extraordinary testi-

mony to the knowledge of Scripture possessed by the Taborites :—" Pudeat Italiæ sacerdotes, quos ne semel quidem
novam legem constat legisse ; apud Taboritas vix muliercu-
lam invenias, quæ de novo Testamento et veteri respondere
nesciat."—" Let the priests of Italy be ashamed, who, it is
well known, have not even once read the New Law ; among
the Taborites you can scarcely find a woman who cannot answer questions on the New and Old Testaments."

Nor will it be altogether uninteresting to add a slight
sketch of the origin of these Bohemian Brethren, from
whom, after the destruction of Bohemian liberty, the present
" Moravians," or " Herrnhuters," took their rise. After the
forcible suppression of Tabor by George Podiebrad, religious
thought was some time before it found itself a home. A
great teacher arose in Peter Chelczicky, whose school at
Unwald was dispersed, and all congregational assemblies
forbidden, while individuals were exposed to the severest
persecution. " Yet," says Palacky, " their number increased,
especially among the lower orders, among peasants and
tradespeople, though a few noblemen and clergymen joined
them ; their very danger increased their resolution as well as
their prudence. Led by Brother Gregory, they from the
first adopted the doctrines of Peter Chelczicky, and made
great exertions to free themselves from the suspicion of wishing to follow the example of the Taborites—a violent sect,
as it appeared to them, which had missed the path of truth
—since, though it understood the law in theory, it dared to
transgress it openly in practice. One of the first manifestoes,
the ' Consent on the Mountains of Reichenau,' (*Swoleni na
horach Rychnowskych*,) in 1464, indicated as the object of
the union, ' The abiding in the righteousness which is from
God ; the leading a virtuous, humble, quiet, self-restrained,
patient, and pure life; the holding fast the Christian faith,

and social intercourse in the spirit of love, and in mutual readiness to aid ;' in order that thereby might be manifest that with them 'faith and love stood without deception, and also certain hope of heaven.' The following resolution is also particularly remarkable :—'We must hold fast to all that is righteous, good, and honourable, wherever and under whatever Government we are, to which we must pay taxes, and render services in humble obedience, and for which we must pray to God. Thus we should also be one with our neighbours in the congregation, and in obedience and union assist everything that is beneficial to the common weal. Thus the brethren and sisters who practise a trade or agriculture, or serve for hire, may seek for gain, in order to supply their wants. The freeholders and landed proprietors may farm their property, and if they understand that a Christian of the same faith is in need, they ought to impart to him of their substance according to his wants ; and thus bearing each other's burthens, all seek to fulfil the law of Christ.' There was nothing in their manifesto which Rokycana, the Utraquist Archbishop Designate of Prague, or the Pope himself, could not have subscribed, just as well as its authors ; for it had no other object than the practice of Christianity, somewhat affected by the socialist spirit of the primitive Church. What, however, drew most odium upon the new 'Brethren' was, the dogma they held, that the sacraments, when administered by priests who led a vicious life, lost their salutary efficacy, and the circumstance that they, on that account, attended only to such clergymen as, in their judgment, lived piously and enjoyed the grace of God. From a public document which they issued, July 29, 1468, we learn, 'That it had been for several years strictly forbidden in Bohemia to hold religious meetings, not only in towns, but also in villages, and even where there were no

priests, and that whether the number attending such meetings were large or small; and that transgressors of this law
were arrested, punished, and imprisoned; but meetings for
evil purposes, whether large or small, were fully permitted.'

"After considerable search and inquiry abroad to find an
ecclesiastical constitution to their mind, and after spending
considerable time in fasting and prayer to ascertain whether
it was God's will that they should proceed, the brethren at
length resolved utterly to renounce the power and authority
of the Pope and his hierarchy, and to introduce amongst
themselves ' an order after the constitution of the primitive
Church.' In the midst of the wars of the year 1467, on a
day which is still unknown, the principal members of the
brotherhood in Bohemia and Moravia met, to the number of
seventy persons, in the village of Lhatka, not far from Reichenau, at the house of a householder named Duchek, who
had not the least knowledge of what was about to happen.
After many prayers, under the direction of Michael, the
parish priest of Lenkenberg, nine men in the company, who
were considered the most worthy, were chosen, and twelve
lots prepared, nine of which were blank, and three signed
with the word 'gest,' 'it is.' A boy named Procop, who
knew nothing whatever about what was going on, distributed
the lots among the nine men, to the share of three of whom,
Mathias of Kunwald, Toma of Przelaucz, and Elias Müller
of Chrzenkow, fell those marked with 'gest.' These men
were then presented to a priest in Romish orders, and one
of the Waldenses, who occupied the position of chief elder
among his co-religionists, in order to be confirmed ' by im-
position of hands after the order of the primitive Church,
and conformably to Apostolic directions.' Next came the
confirmation itself in the case of all three, and, in that of
one of the three, assumption of the first rank in the authority

of the priestly office. After this, both Rokycana and King George proceeded to severe measures against the brethren, and the matter was being deliberated at the Parliament at Beneschau, when an invasion by Mathias Corvinus, King of Hungary, drew the attention of both king and council to war and arms, rather than to religion and internal affairs."

Here Palacky's history leaves us, and, if the variations in later times between the authentic and current history of Bohemia are as great as those which he has pointed out, it will be but little use attempting more than the briefest summary of events.

Two rivals now contended for the Bohemian crown, Mathias Corvinus, the King of Hungary, and the Polish Prince Wladislaw, the former of whom was favoured by the Pope and the Catholic party, the latter by the Utraquists. Wladislaw was elected by the Parliament, in accordance with the wishes of the deceased monarch, and, after considerable struggles with both sword and pen, an arrangement was made between the rivals, under which the survivor was to succeed to the possessions of the other, if he died without legitimate heirs. Wladislaw succeeded to the crown of Hungary, and died in 1516, leaving both kingdoms to his son Lewis, a boy of ten years of age. Jordan mentions, as one reason for the election of Wladislaw as King of Bohemia, that he was perfect master of the Bohemian language, *it being at that time the court language in Poland.* Lewis perished in the battle of Mohacz, gained by the Turks in 1524.

In the reign of Lewis, during which the government was carried on rather by the Parliament and native statesmen than by the king, Luther's doctrines began to enter into Bohemia. This caused a rising against the Catholic clergy, and threatened a schism among the Bohemians them-

selves, which was quickly put an end to by the choice of
Hawel Czahera, the Lutheran leader, to the administrator-
ship of the Utraquists, and the prohibition of all sects in
the country except the Utraquist and Catholic confessions.
Nevertheless, the Bohemian Brethren maintained their
ground, in spite of difficulties, and even persecutions, in the
districts of Jungbunzlau and Königgrätz, and in Moravia;
and their literary activity was most remarkable. The first
book printed in Bohemia was in Latin, and appeared at
Pilsen in 1476; the Psalter was printed in Bohemian in
1487; and the whole Bible in 1488, and a second edition
followed in 1489. Of all the printing establishments that of
the brethren was the most active and important, and the result of their efforts was that the Bohemians were the best
read nation in Europe at that day.

Ferdinand of Austria, brother of the Emperor Charles V,
and husband of Anna the daughter of the late Bohemian
king Wladislaw, was elected King of Bohemia on Oct. 24,
1526. The Utraquist Consistory at Prague was renewed,
the Anabaptists expelled from the country, and the remarkable law introduced that no landowner might prevent a serf
or retainer from devoting himself in a regular manner to
scientific study. But Ferdinand conceived and carried out
but too successfully a bloody conspiracy against the liberties
of his kingdom, which nearly reduced it to the level of the
German despotisms, whether large or small, which then in-
fested and have not yet ceased to infest the continent of Europe. He also introduced the Jesuits into Bohemia, in 1556,
in order to oppose the Utraquist professors of the University of Prague, and they soon became the richest and most
powerful order in the country, and devoted their entire energy
to bringing about a reactionary revolution in the political
and literary circumstances of the Bohemian nation. The

only good action of Ferdinand's, as regards Bohemia, was his application to Pope Pius IV. to sanction the use of the cup in the communion by the laity, and to reconsider the question of the celibacy of the clergy, the latter of which requests was put off with an evasive answer, while the former was granted in 1564, in hopes of the eventual return of the Utraquists into the bosom of the Holy Roman Church.

Ferdinand died in the same year, and was succeeded by his son Maximilian, who, in return for the liberal aid voted by the Bohemian Parliament for the Turkish war, suspended the " Compactata," and proclaimed an universal toleration for each and every religious Confession in 1567.

Maximilian died on Oct. 12, 1575, and was succeeded by his son the Emperor Rudolf II. Peace had hitherto been maintained between the different religious parties by the Catholic Archbishop of Prague, Antonius of Müglitz, after whose death, in 1580, a different spirit became dominant. His successor almost immediately induced Rudolf illegally to proclaim the banishment of the Bohemian Brethren from the country, and they were, in fact, compelled to keep themselves completely in the background. In 1584, Rudolf, with the consent of the Parliament, introduced the new Gregorian Calendar, into Bohemia, and at the same time, of his own authority, commanded the names of the national martyrs, Hus and Jerome, to be erased from the calendar. In 1602 the " Compactata " were again revived by Rudolf in the narrowest sense, and none but Catholics and Utraquists were allowed to hold any public worship. In 1603 the school of the Bohemian Brethren at Bunzlau was destroyed, so that the Jesuits had, henceforth, no antagonist of moment but the Utraquist University of Prague. Nevertheless, on July 5, 1609, the Parliament extorted a solemn charter re-establishing complete religious freedom. Rudolf's brother,

Mathias, rebelled against him in Hungary and Austria, compelled him to abdicate, and was crowned King of Bohemia,
amidst universal joy, on May 23, 1611.

The thirty-six years of the reign of Rudolf are called the
golden age of Bohemian literature, as the king was both a
learned student, especially of chemistry and natural philosophy, himself, and encouraged learning in every branch.
Tycho Brahe and Kepler were invited to his court, and the
faculty of medicine at Prague boasted some of the most distinguished chemists and engineers of the age. A specimen of
the prose writers of this date, literally, and I fear too literally,
translated, is now offered to the English public, in hopes that
it will draw attention not only to the past, but also to the
important present and promising future of the Bohemians,
especially of that remnant of the Hussites which is now
rapidly increasing in both number and cultivation. But the
most remarkable feature in Bohemia at that time was the
excellence of the local schools, one of which existed, according to Pelzel, in every little market-town in both Bohemia
and Moravia. In Prague there were sixteen such schools,
while Kuttenberg and Jungbunzlau possessed two each.
None of these possessed fewer than two teachers, and many
had four, five, or even six. No one was allowed to become a
schoolmaster till he had taken the B.A. degree in the Caro-
linum at Prague. Thus many citizens were to be found in
the towns who were well acquainted with Virgil, Ovid, and
Horace, and even with Homer and Anacreon, and who wrote
Latin and Greek poetry themselves. If a professor was
wanted in the University, he was sought amongst the best of
the schoolmasters in the country.

With Mathias the literary and scientific glory of Bohemia
declined. His great endeavour was to obtain men and money
for his wars in Hungary, and he therefore allowed the Parlia-

ment to take its own measures for securing the nationality and national language. But he supported every aggression on the part of the Romish priesthood and Jesuits against the Utraquists and others, and finally obtained the coronation of Ferdinand of Styria, in 1607, as his successor in Bohemia. Soon afterwards the Bohemian liberties were so plainly infringed by the Romish clergy, and justice so flatly refused by the king, that on May 23, 1618, his two principal councillors, Martinitz and Slawata, were thrown out of the window by the infuriated Utraquist Parliament, which, three days afterwards, nominated thirty directors with full powers, and soon afterwards issued an edict banishing, within fourteen days, the "poisonous order," the "hypocritical, dangerous, and turbulent sect of the Jesuits," from the kingdom. After several victories had been gained by the Bohemians over the imperial forces, and negotiations been begun, which promised to lead to a favourable issue, Mathias died, on March 20, 1619.

Ferdinand had already extirpated Lutheranism out of Styria, where it had been professed by the majority of the people; the Bohemians, therefore, refused to recognize him as their king, on the plea that he had already broken his coronation oath. Ferdinand, however, was elected emperor by the German electors, in spite of the efforts of some of the Protestant princes. Frederic, the Elector of the Palatinate, was chosen king, and crowned at Prague with his wife Elizabeth, the daughter of James I. of England, by the administrator of the Utraquist Consistory, and in the course of the winter received the homage of the Estates of Moravia. Frederic and his religious advisers, being strong Calvinists, soon came into collision with the prejudices of the Utraquists, who were still more nearly allied to the Catholics than the Lutherans, and in the excess of their zeal went so far as to commit the most glaring violations of the Charter, which secured perfect religious freedom to all parties. Another foolish act was the deposition of the two generals Thurn and Mansfelt, who had signalised themselves by a series of victories, and the elevation of a couple of particularly incompetent strangers into their places. The result was the complete defeat of the Bohemian army, on Nov. 8, 1620, at the White Mountain, a few miles from Prague, a defeat which was not retarded by the obstinate refusal of Frederic to favour his army with his presence until he had had his dinner. He fled immediately on receiving the news of the defeat, and Prague was soon in the hands of the imperialists.

Then came the day of blood,—the 21st of June, 1621,— when twenty-seven of Bohemia's best and noblest perished on the scaffold. The Bohemian Brethren and Calvinists were immediately banished from the country, and in Feb. 1622, the Utraquist and Lutheran clergy at Prague were offered the alternatives of giving up their wives and receiving a fresh ordination, or leaving Bohemia. On June 18, 1623, the stone-chalice, overlaid with gold, was taken down from the Teyn church at Prague, and the bones of the Utraquist Archbishop Elect, Rokycana, publicly burnt. Crowds of monks were introduced from Spain, Italy, and other Catholic countries. In the spring of 1626 a decree was published to the following effect:—No one who refused to profess the Catholic religion might carry on any trade, business, or profession. No preaching, baptisms, or marriages were allowed in any house, and it was punishable with death to harbour any evangelical clergyman; the non-Catholic dead were not to be buried by Catholic priests, but the burial fees were to be paid for them all the same; any one convicted of holding any heretical service in his house must leave the country; all children were to be withdrawn from non-Catholic schools, and all domestic instruction was strictly forbidden; no non-Catholic could make a valid will; and none but Catholic boys might be taken as apprentices. The Jesuits traversed the country with soldiers to protect them, in order to carry out these measures with the utmost severity. The poorer classes thus driven from their homes rose in rebellion, but were either cut to pieces on the spot, or taken prisoners, and then broken on the wheel, hung, beheaded, branded with redhot irons on the forehead, or deprived of their noses and ears. Nevertheless, many thousands fled into the forests, where they retained the faith of their fathers for a century and a-half, till better times enabled them to profess it openly. In the autumn of 1627, Ferdinand came to Prague with his empress and son, and formally deprived the Bohemian Estates of all important rights and privileges, except that of granting supplies in the way of taxes, a right which they have never been permitted to exercise. More than 36,000 noble families left or were driven from Bohemia, and its conversion to Holy Mother Church was effected by the reduction of the number of its inhabitants from about 4,000,000 to about 800,000.

From this time forth Bohemia slept a deep and terrible sleep, and history is not concerned with the doings but the sufferings of the Bohemian people. Soon came the devastations of the thirty-years' war to add themselves to the destruction of the national literature and suppression of the national intellect, which had been so eagerly pushed forwards by those " enemies of the human race," the Jesuits.

The feelings of Bohemians towards this death-sleep of their country are very striking. Last summer I met a Bohemian gentleman who addressed me thus :—" Sir, you are come to visit a dead and buried and forgotten nation." But a translation of the beautiful dedication of Erben's " Kytice," or

" Nosegay," of national tales, in which he takes advantage of the fact that, in Bohemian and several other Slavonic dialects, a pretty little wild flower is called the " Mother's soul," will probably be the most attractive means of exhibiting these patriotic feelings to the English eye.

> A mother had died and was laid in the grave,
>   Her orphans still stayed here,
> And every morning together they went
>   And sought for their mother dear.
>
> The mother was woe for her children dear,
>   Back came the soul that was fled,
> And embodied itself in a tiny flower,
>   Which soon the grave o'erspread.
>
> The children their mother knew again
>   By the scent so sweet around,
> And their mother's soul they call'd the flower,
>   Wherein they comfort found.
>
> O mother's soul of my country dear—
>   Tales simple enough, I trow—
> I gather'd thee on an ancient grave,
>   To whom shall I give thee now ?
>
> In a tiny nosegay thy flowers I'll twine,
>   With a band I'll fairly bind,
> I'll point thee the way to the lands so wide,
>   Where kindred thou wilt find.
>
> Some daughter of her mother perhaps will be there,
>   To whom thy scent will be sweet,
> Perhaps, too, some son of thy mother thou'lt find,
>   Whose heart thy flowers will greet.

In 1773 the dissolution of the order of the Jesuits took place, and in 1781, the first year of his reign, the Emperor Joseph II. issued the celebrated Patent of Toleration, allowing free liberty of conscience and worship to all non-Catholics. Relics of the old sects sprang up immediately, so that they numbered more than 100,000 souls in Bohemia

and Moravia. Some of these sectaries entertained very
singular, and, indeed, outrageous doctrines, so that measures
were taken to limit the toleration to the Lutheran, or Evangelical, and Reformed, or Zwinglian Confessions. In 1782
followed the dissolution of all monasteries and convents,
which were not engaged either in giving school instruction,
or in the care of the sick.

The great majority of the Bohemian and Moravian Protestants belong to the Helvetian Confession, but do not de-
rive their traditions from Zwingle or Calvin, but from the
Hussite and other writers of their own country. According
to the latest authorities, the number of Lutherans in Bohemia—exclusive of the purely German Inspectorate of Asch,
which was established by a peculiar patent in 1775, and now
contains 17,000 souls—is 15,685, who are pretty equally
divided between the German and Bohemian languages,
while the Reformed number no less than 59,343, all recog-
nizing and using in public worship the Bohemian language
only. In Moravia, the statistics of which I do not possess
to a later date than 1851, there were then 19,433 Lutherans,
and 34,932 Reformed; in Galicia, 27,481 Lutherans, and
1,882 Reformed; and in Austrian Silesia, no less than
62,463 Lutherans, most of them speaking the Silesian dialect
of the Polish language.

The Gustavus-Adolphus Society—that brightest of bright
spots in Protestant Germany—a society which extends its
fostering care over all struggling Protestant congregations in
non-Protestant countries, arose to a great extent out of circumstances connected with Bohemia. The Protestant inhabitants of the Bohemian village of Fleissen had, since
the Patent of Toleration, been ecclesiastically united as one
parish with those of the Saxon village of Brambach, enjoying the benefit of the same clergyman, and the same schools.

Suddenly orders came from Vienna that this intercourse must cease, and the poor Protestants of Fleissen must find a clergyman, and build a church and schoolhouse for themselves. The representations of the Saxon government were of no avail. Just at this time the German Protestants were celebrating the 200th anniversary of the death of Gustavus Adolphus of Sweden at Lützen, in 1632, and Dr. Grossmann, of Leipsic, bethought himself of the idea of a society for the assistance of struggling Protestant congregations, which is now being so magnificently carried out, and appears on the stage of the world as a worthy rival of the great English Bible and Missionary Societies.

This excellent society has assisted several congregations in Bohemia, both Lutherans and Reformed; and last year one of its agents travelled through Bohemia and Moravia with a view to the furtherance of its objects in those countries. The result of his journey has appeared in the October number of the *Protestantische Monatsblätter* of 1861. The writer of this article draws particular attention to the entire freedom from Rationalism enjoyed by these Slavonic churches, and to the fact that nothing but the most strictly Scriptural doctrine is heard from their pulpits, or would be endured by the congregations. He laments the poor and dependent position of the Protestant clergy, and also the great difficulty which they have in procuring a regular academical or theological education. Owing to the expense of and difficulty in obtaining such an education, and also owing to the dependent position of the clergy, as paid entirely by their congregations, it has come to pass that there are now four Reformed benefices vacant in Bohemia, and only two young men studying as candidates of theology. If they become salaried by the Government, their offensive power against the mass of Popery would be gone, and they would be looked

upon as mere Government officials, and would, besides, lose
the presents and contributions in kind which they at present
receive in addition to their little salaries of 30*l.* or 40*l.* a-
year. What course, therefore, remains but to endeavour to
raise a fund which shall provide small endowments in aid
both of young men seeking to prepare themselves for Holy
Orders, and for the duties of schoolmasters, and of the miserably underpaid clergy and schoolmasters themselves. The
death of Szafarzik, the Protestant archæologist and philo-
loger last year evoked a burst of enthusiasm, and both
Catholics and Protestants vied in subscribing towards the
foundation of a seminary for the Protestant clergy, to be
erected as a memorial of him. Next year (1863) is the
1,000th anniversary of the introduction of Christianity into
these Slavonic countries, and a grand effort will be made by
both Catholics and Protestants to turn this heart-stirring
jubilee to their own account. It rests, under God, with
foreign Protestants to leave their poor Bohemian and Moravian brethren to be overwhelmed by the wealth and numbers of their opponents, or to lend them a helping hand,
and render them victorious in the contest.

And victorious they will be, if they obtain but a moderate
amount of aid. They have the glorious past of their country,
and all the best feelings of nationality on their side. They
can say,—Our country always flourished among the first in
Europe, so long as it kept the Pope and his crew at arm's
length; when once Popery and its hordes came in, the sun
of Bohemia set in blood, and a death-trance succeeded the
life and energy which had defied and successfully resisted
the whole might of Roman Catholic Europe.

Last year I, too, visited Bohemia on a similar errand on
my own account, and I can most fully testify to the accuracy
of every statement made by the excellent author of the article

to which I have just referred. I found the Protestants in considerable excitement, and just conducting the elections of Presbyteries, &c. required by the New Patent of April 8, 1861, which freed them from the old consistory at Vienna, presided over by a Roman Catholic, and granted them a free ecclesiastical constitution, and perfect freedom of action in religious matters. I found that one Reformed clergyman had received no less than 449 Romanists into his flock, and that the young Reformed congregation at Prague had increased in thirteen years from 800 to 1,600. And to the Biblical doctrine and preaching of the Bohemian clergy I can bear the fullest witness from the testimony of my own ears.

Two editions of Archbishop Whately's *Easy Lessons on Christian Evidences* have been published in Bohemian by the Rev. Josef Prochazka, and I saw myself the proof-sheets of the *Second Epistle of St. Peter* in an edition of the Scriptures with the Apocrypha which was being carried through the press by the Rev. Josef Ruzicka, a Lutheran clergyman at Prague. Everything betokens life and hope. There is a society well deserving of aid at Leschitz, for the assistance of the widows and orphans of clergymen and schoolmasters, without distinction of confession. And the same place is honourably distinguished by its lending library, which has transformed the congregation, mentally and morally, into quite a different class of people. This possesses above 600 volumes, and the peasants of the neighbourhood club together to purchase candles, take books out for a nominal sum—Catholics as well as Protestants—and read together by turns in each other's cottages during the long winter evenings.

Will England remain uninterested and indifferent at this approaching jubilee? England, from whose Wycliffe came the enlightenment that, by God's grace, enabled Hus and Jerome to give their bodies to be burned at Constance? The little flame which arose, in 1781, out of the long and cruelly smothered embers of the torch thus transmitted from England to Bohemia, is now becoming larger and larger, and brighter and brighter, and promises to burst into a sun-bright splendour of religious enlightenment, if not neglected by those who ought to interest themselves in it. And the rapidity with which constitutions have been solemnly promulgated and as solemnly revoked, with which concessions have been made on paper and annulled with a stroke of the pen in Austria, must surely show the absolute necessity of immediately realizing and consolidating everything that has been granted. It would seem as if it were now or never. Will England resume her ancient work of aid and enlightenment in favour of these long oppressed, but now liberated, zealous and deserving fellow-Protestants?

A. H. WRATISLAW.

ADVENTURES OF BARON WENCESLAS WRATISLAW.

BOOK I.

Wherein is contained the Journey of the Imperial Embassy from Vienna to Constantinople.

 WENCESLAS* WRATISLAW of *Mitrowitz* was entrusted by my relatives to the care of *Frederic Kregwitz,* who was sent to Constantinople with rich presents, in the year 1591, by his Majesty the Roman Emperor *Rudolph II,* as Ambassador Extraordinary to the Turkish Emperor, Sultan *Amurath III.* The object of my relatives was, that I should gain experience and see eastern countries. We spent several months of that year at Vienna, waiting till the jewellery, watches, and other special presents, which our ambassa-

---

* *Wacleslaw* or *Waclaw* is the Bohemian ; *Wenceslaw* is the Polish name ; and *Wenceslas* or *Wenceslaus* is the Latinized form best known in England.

dor was to offer, not only to the Turkish emperor, but
also to his pashas and grandees, were brought from
Augsburg; and in the meantime the ambassador provided himself with the barges on which we were to
sail to Comorn, and with other necessaries appertaining
to the journey.

When everything was in readiness, and had been
brought to Vienna, *Herr von Kregwitz*, with all who
were to travel to Constantinople, had a final audience
of his Imperial Majesty and the Archduke Ernest.
After kissing his Majesty's hand, on Sept. 2, 1591, we
took leave of our friends, embarked in our boats, and
sailed down the Danube to an Austrian town called
Wissamund, four German miles from Vienna.   There
an Austrian gentleman named *Unverzagt* (Dauntless)
awaited us.   We went to his chateau, where he received and entertained us with great hospitality.   In
this town we stayed two days, as some letters and
collateral presents, which we were to distribute in the
Turkish court, were still unprepared, and had not been
sent to us.

When all was ready we left Wissamund for Comorn,
on Sept. 4.   Thence a message was sent in the morning
to Mahomed Beg at Gran, and notice given of the
arrival of the ambassador, in order that he might send
as soon as possible boats and an escort to meet us for
our better security.   Meanwhile we were entertained
by Herr Erasmus Braun, the mayor of Comorn.   After
dinner we walked about the town and inspected the
fortress.   Here we stayed for seven days, at the end of
which intelligence came that the Turks were waiting to
receive us, at the usual place, in a beautiful plain ; we

therefore set out from Comorn, our *cortège* on land
consisting of about 300 foot-soldiers, under a captain,
without firearms, and only with sidearms, and about
fifty hussars on horseback; on the Danube we had
fifteen boats, each carrying three guns and twenty-five
Hungarian soldiers with long muskets, javelins, and
their pennons. Thus we voyaged some hours down the
Danube, till we espied the Turkish boats, which were
ten in number.

The Turkish boats were exactly similar to ours in all
respects, except in carrying only one gun each. On
land about one hundred very fine-looking and well-
appointed Turkish horsemen rode towards us, and, on
perceiving us, set spurs to their horses and galloped to
the very brink of the Danube. Herr von Kregwitz
then ordered the boats to cast anchor. We disembarked on the bank and welcomed and were welcomed
by our Turkish friends, and ere long partook of dinner
together in the boats. It was certainly matter of wonder,
to a person who had never beheld anything of the kind
before, to see the beautiful horses, the lances with streaming pennons, the sabres inlaid with silver, gold, and precious stones, the magnificent cloths of blue and red, the
gilded saddles and caparisons of the Turks; and I think
they must have equipped themselves in this manner on
purpose. While the principal Turks were dining with
the ambassador the hussars of both parties walked on
the plain and conversed together in a friendly manner,
their horses and lances being held by *jermeks* or grooms.
Here a quarrel arose between a Turkish hussar and one
of ours. They wanted to break a lance on the spot,
which, however, was strictly forbidden by their officers,

and they deferred the matter till such time as they should meet in battle. They were both very eager to try each other's strength, but, though we should have liked to see the fight, we did not allow them to proceed to such extremities.

After dinner we took leave of our Christian friends, and placed ourselves under the protection of the Turks. Lashing their boats to ours, they towed us down the Danube as far as Gran. Here Mahomet the *sangiak* (so called from a banner on the top of which is a gilt horsetail, the ensign of knighthood) sent us three janissaries, as a guard for our protection.

The janissaries are much regarded in all the Turkish dominions, as being the Turkish emperor's household troops. They are infantry, and attend on the Sultan's person, to the number of 12,000; the rest are dispersed through almost all his territories; whether placed in castles and fortresses as garrisons against enemies, or stationed for the protection of the Jews and Christians against the illegal violence of the mob. They wear long garments down to the instep, but of cloth, not of silk, which never comes upon them. Instead of hats they wear a kind of sleeves, into the wider end of which they put their heads ; these are different at each end, and one end hangs down the neck as far as the back, whereas there is a tube of silver gilt, set with pearls and the more ordinary precious stones, in front over the forehead. In this in war time they place feathers.

These janissaries are for the most part kidnapped persons, or children of Christian peasants living under the Turkish sway. Some hundreds of these latter are assembled every third year, bringing with them their male children of eight, nine, or ten years old. Surgeons are on the spot, who judge of the mental capacity of each individual child from his personal appearance, and determine for what future occupation he is likely to be fit. The most promising are selected for the service of the Turkish emperor, the next class for that of the pashas and other Turkish officials; the remainder, who appear of less intellectual promise, are sold into Anatolia or Asia, to any one who chooses to purchase them, for a ducat each. There they are kept till the appointed time, *i. e.* till they are eighteen, or, at latest, twenty years old; are brought up in want, poverty, cold, and heat, and are altogether treated little better than dogs: only whoever takes such a boy is obliged to bring him back again to the Sultan's court at the expiration of the above period, should the kidnapped youth still be living; should he die, his master must report the fact to the cadi or judge of the district, who keeps a register of such boys, in order that he may be struck out of the list. When about twenty years old, all embrowned with sun and heat, and accustomed to all kinds of labour, they are brought to Constantinople from the different countries in which they have thus been dispersed. There the most active are enrolled as *acziam oglany*, or young janissaries, and assigned to veteran janissaries to learn, under their instruction, to shoot, to use the sabre, to fling darts, to leap over trenches, and to scale walls. They are bound to obey every order given by the elder janissaries, to prepare their food, cleave wood, and perform every necessary service as long as peace lasts. When they march with the elder soldiers to war, although enrolled in their number, they are still obliged to wait upon them, to pitch their tents, and to look after the camels and mules which carry their provisions and necessaries. On occasion of a battle or skirmish they march in the van, and endeavour to surpass each other in valour and steadiness; nor are any of these boys taken into the number of the veteran janissaries till they have borne themselves like heroes. The younger are then bound to serve and attend upon them, as they did previously upon others. From these it is that the bravest and fiercest warriors that the Turks possess arise, and it is on these that the Turkish emperor places the greatest reliance. I have written this account of the janissaries, in recording the first occasion on which I saw them, because I was afterwards an eyewitness at Constantinople of the manner in which, from youth upwards, they are obliged to accustom themselves, not to pleasure, but to work, and are formed into the formidable soldiers which they are. I saw them here for the first time, when they kissed my lord the ambassador's hands, and presented themselves for his service.

It was already late, so that we were unable to enter into any business on his Imperial Majesty's behalf with the sangiak. He, however, gave orders to provide us with a sufficient supply of meat, wine, sturgeon, fish, and fowls. Here, having no feather-beds or mattresses, we for the first time began to lie on carpets and rugs, with which each prepared himself a place of repose for the night as he best could.

Early in the morning of Sept. 8 the sangiak sent to the boats fifteen extremely handsome Turkish horses, with splendid housings and saddles, all studded with

silver, gilt, and embroidered with precious stones and
pearls. These were mounted and ridden in procession
by those gentlemen of equestrian rank who were accompanying the ambassador to Constantinople. After
them walked the servants, two and two, bearing presents for the sangiak. Next came four boys of equestrian rank, who carried weapons before my lord the
ambassador. The first bore a sabre overlaid with silver
and gilt, with its scabbard set with pearls and precious
stones ; the second, a *buzygan* or mace,* overlaid
with silver and gilt, and set with precious stones; the
third, a Hungarian battle-axe, with its handle also set
with precious stones; and the fourth carried a Hungarian morgenstern,† splendidly ornamented with precious stones, and gilt all over. After these rode the
ambassador on a very beautiful Turkish horse, white
as snow,‡ followed by his steward or major-domo.

After riding for some time we came in sight of the
sangiak's abode, which was a common unpretending
house. On arriving the ambassador went immediately
upstairs, and we followed him. There the sangiak
gave audience to the ambassador, and bade him sit
down on a chair opposite himself. Round the sangiak
stood his principal councillors and warriors, and we
posted ourselves behind the ambassador. When the
ambassador delivered his Imperial Majesty's letter to
the sangiak, the latter received it with due reverence
and resumed his seat. The ambassador then delivered

* With a pear-shaped head, almost like a hammer, according to
Jungman.
† A kind of mace studded with sharp points at the end.
‡ Literally, " chalk."

to him the presents from his Imperial Majesty, viz.
300 broad doubloons, a silver-gilt beaker, and a silver-
gilt ewer and basin.

When this business was ended, permission was given
us to go and see the Castle of Gran, in which the archbishop formerly lived. On entering the church, in
which the Turks perform their devotions, we saw a
handsome chapel, cased inside with marble, in which
was a beautiful representation of the Annunciation of
the Virgin Mary, made of variegated marble. Thence
we ascended by a lofty staircase into a handsome private
chapel, in which were pictures of saints. Next to this
chapel was a tolerably spacious palace, and in it pictures
of the former kings of Hungary. Immediately behind
the palace is a beautiful gallery, adorned all round with
marble pillars, from which there is an extensive view of
the fields and plains, as well as of the city, which is
close to the Danube. Under this gallery is an extraordinary well, hewn out of the solid rock, and so deep
that, when a stone is thrown into it, the splash cannot
be heard for a considerable time. The water is forced
up from the Danube at a vast expense. The well is a
very beautiful one, and must have cost the Hungarian
archbishop, who formerly had his usual abode here,
many thousand ducats. After seeing what there was
in the fortress, we repaired to our boats and dined.
After dinner we started again down the Danube with
our escort, i.e. with the ten boats, to which ours were
lashed. We sailed past the Castle Wyssehrad,* which
is situated on a lofty eminence, and towards evening
arrived at Waitzen, where also a bishop's see formerly

* High castle.

existed. Although no bishop lives there, they informed us that his revenues were regularly paid him.

We started again early on Sept. 9, and in three hours were in sight of Buda. On our arriving within about half-a-mile of the place the pasha sent nineteen barges, or ships, in excellent condition, and ornamented with flags, to meet us. These, on coming up to us, fired all their guns, both great and small, and our boats answered them in like manner; this was repeated several times. It was a wondrous spectacle when these nine-and-twenty boats placed themselves cross-wise on the Danube, and that with so many pennons, flags, and pendants, like a field of poppies in flower. There were full 700 of these on the boats, and our eyes were greatly delighted at the sight. When we approached close to Buda all the boats fired again and drew to the shore, where the pasha of Buda had given orders for us to be well supplied with provisions and necessaries, and a guard of janissaries to be assigned us.

In the morning of Sept. 10 the pasha sent down to the boats sixteen beautiful horses, splendidly caparisoned with saddles, stirrups, and other furniture richly gilt. These were mounted by the ambassador and those of his attendants who enjoyed the rank of knights. They rode off in the same manner as they had done at Gran. All the way from the suburb to the pasha's abode stood soldiers in rows on both sides, and we rode through the midst of them. On arriving at the pasha's house we found 200 janissaries stationed between the entrance and the staircase, as a kind of body-guard. On entering the entrance-hall we saw the pasha sitting in the midst of valuable carpets upon a divan. Round him sat his principal chiaouses, councillors, and chief officers, the rest standing. Opposite the pasha was a red velvet chair, in which the ambassador took his seat after giving his hand to the pasha, and about fifteen of us, who were present, stood behind the ambassador. The whole of the audience hall, spacious as it was, had the floor covered with handsome carpets and the walls hung with tapestry.

When Herr von Kregwitz delivered the letter from his Imperial Majesty to the pasha, the latter rose up, kissed the letter, placed it on his head or turban, and afterwards held it in his hand. The ambassador then delivered him the present, viz. 300 broad dollars, two large crescent-shaped silver bottles, a silver-gilt ewer and basin, and a very handsome striking-clock. After presenting these gifts he conversed for a considerable time with the pasha, and made complaints of certain Turkish soldiers, who had done us injury by carrying off cattle, demanding that this should be put a stop to and prohibited for the future. The ambassador also delivered to him a letter from Ernest, archduke of Austria, which he received politely, though not so reverentially, as that from the Emperor. We remained full three hours, while this business was being transacted. The pasha presented the ambassador in return with a Turkish caftan, or overcoat, of gold brocade, which he immediately put on, in token of acknowledgment, and rode wearing it to the boat.

On returning to the boats we learnt that one of our company, an Italian named Nicholas de Bello, a native of the island of Crete or Candy, had turned Turk. This person had been brought by the ambassador from

Vienna at his own most earnest desire; he declared
that he had a brother in captivity among the Turks,
whom he wished to ransom and bring by sea back to
Christendom, and thus save his soul. While we were
at the pasha's this Italian left the boat in which he
was and went to the janissaries, who had been assigned
us as a guard, whose tents were pitched on a hill near
the Danube. There he drank and made acquaintance
with them, and gave them to understand that he wanted
to become a Turk, by taking his hat from his head,
treading it under foot, cutting it to pieces, and finally
throwing it into the Danube; he also tore his collar
to pieces. As soon as he had done this the janissaries
brought him a turban or round Turkish cap, placed it
upon his head, and conducted him into the town. This
Italian had started most devoutly upon the journey,
and often used to sigh and bewail his brother's ruin, till
tears streamed from his eyes; then, however, the cunning villain forgot his own soul and became a Mahometan, though, previously to our beginning our voyage
down the Danube, he had confessed and received the
most holy sacrament of the altar.

The same day the pasha sent a very handsome boat
for the ambassador to visit him in, which he did, taking
with him only five persons. He carried with him a
beautifully ornamented gun, and a large white English
dog, a present from his Highness the Archduke Ernest,
both which he gave the pasha.

Meanwhile, whilst the ambassador stayed transacting
business with the pasha, we visited and bathed in the
warm baths, which were not far from our boats. These
are certainly remarkably pleasant, so warm that one

can scarcely sit down in them, and flowing spontaneously from a natural spring.   The Turks say that,
being thus naturally warm without the use of artificial
means, they are extremely salubrious.   Care is taken
to keep them clean, and every one who uses them has
all requisite attendance and comfort for a moderate
sum of money.   In front of the bath is a large saloon,
with a broad bench all round it, where the bathers un-
dress and leave their clothes.   In the middle of this
saloon stand several broadish marble cisterns, out of
which you go into the bathhouse.   This is much more
like a circular chapel than a bath, being ornamented
outside with sheet-lead and variegated marble, and
paved and inlaid inside, both walls and floor.   Inter-
nally the bath is like a tub, forty-three paces in circumference, and the water in it is deep enough to reach the
chin of a middle-sized man.   If any one does not wish
to stand so deep in the water, there are two marble
benches in the bath at his service, one higher than the
other; thus you can sit on the one with the water up
to your armpits, on the second with it up to your waist,
and on the third, which is the rim, with it up to your
knees.   If you wish to swim and amuse yourself, there
is ample space for the purpose.   There are also nine
circular side-rooms with two marble cisterns in each.
By the wall are tin taps or cocks by which you can let
hot or cold water into the cisterns.   There is also provision for letting the water out again.   In a word, we
saw many such amusing and agreeable baths in Turkey
and enjoyed the use of them.

There are, moreover, at the side of this bathhouse two
other small bathhouses, also of a circular form, in which

impotent, sick, and poor people are allowed to bathe and make themselves comfortable. The water is let out of the baths or tubs every night. They are then carefully cleaned out, and clean water is let in in the morning; a matter to which the Turks pay particular attention. If it is discovered in the least that the bath-keeper has not kept the place properly clean, or has neglected to let the water off every night, he comes in for considerable punishment. A case of this I saw with my own eyes at Constantinople, when a bath-keeper opposite our house—it was said in the imperial bath—was convicted of giving people dirty towels, and was punished as follows by the sub-pasha or supreme judge. That official ordered him to be beaten with a stick, and to receive a thousand blows, *i. e.* 200 on the back, 300 on the soles of the feet, 200 on the calves of the legs, and 300 on the stomach. After this he was completely swollen up, just like a newly-hatched pigeon, and no one could have told from his appearance whether he was a human being or no. Some may think this incredible and improbable, but it is really nothing more than the truth. Indeed, when I was in prison, I again saw 1,000 blows given to a German, an account of which I shall give below.

There is an innumerable multitude of these baths in Servia, Thrace, and other parts of the Turkish dominions; and I have mentioned how beautiful and clean they are in order that the reader may form some idea of their exceeding cleanliness: for the Turks, regulating their lives according to the Koran, are obliged to bathe every day. Indeed, the women make an exception in favour of the use of the bath at marriage,

and it is then specially covenanted that their husbands
shall not prevent their going to their baths, which
the men dare not enter under pain of death. They
obtain this privilege upon the ground that a command
is given upon the subject by the Prophet Mahomet, and
that wómen are bound to have a special love of cleanliness.

On Friday, Oct. 11,* a day which the Turks hallow
like our Sunday, we saw the pasha go to divine
worship with great pomp. First rode about 300 janissaries, then a number of chiaouses, and then came some
hundred spahis or foot-soldiers. After these rode the
pasha himself in a dress of gold brocade. He remained
about two hours in the temple, and then returned home
with a similar procession.

After dinner we went up into the town, which, as
well as the castle, is situated on a hill with the Danube
on the right hand, and there are ancient Hungarian
buildings still standing in it. It would be tedious to
write an account of this town; I will only notice what
I saw myself. The town of Buda is situated in an
extremely agreeable and pleasant spot, in a very fertile
and fruitful region, and is built on a rocky hill, so that
vineyards adjoin it on one side, while on the other there
is a view of the Danube, and beyond the Danube you
see the town of Pesth. Behind and around it lie wide and
extensive plains, where there was a certain spot specially
chosen for the election of the kings of Hungary. In
the suburbs of Buda splendid houses were formerly

* The month here changes in the original from *Zari*, September,
to *Rijen*, October; the German translator has *Weinmonat*, October,
throughout.

built, in which the king and other chief magnates of
Hungary used to live; but these have now partly fallen
and been destroyed, or are partly propped up by beams,
and in these latter nobody lives but Turkish soldiers.
These soldiers have no more pay *per diem* than is absolutely necessary for fodder, food, and drink; neither
have they to make arrangements and preparations for
those purposes at home. If it rains in anywhere through
the roof, they pay but little attention thereto, if there
be but a place where they can put their horses and place
their own beds in the dry; hence it comes that houses
and palaces are not easily found in all the Turkish
empire, except in the chief cities, and then they belong to the pashas and principal officials, who alone
possess handsomely built and furnished houses, the
common people usually living in cottages and huts.
The great lords and pashas lay out large sums on gardens, baths, and fine horses, on women and clothes, and
their retainers also erect a house for themselves, in order
to obtain shelter and security.

As we walked in the town past a Turkish church
we saw ten Turks in a circle, holding each other by the
hand, and a priest standing in the midst of them. The
priest and the rest turned and twisted round, crying,
with a loud voice, " Allahu," as though they were saying, " O God, hear us," till it echoed again; and this
they continued doing till they were hoarse. The Turks
say that, whenever any one falls asleep during this
screaming, whatever he dreams is considered as a kind
of prophecy; and it is acknowledged that this is very
truth, and reveals itself at its proper time.

In the town we went into a Christian church, where

there was a Calvinistic preacher instead of a regular parson. Attached to that church is a tolerably high tower, in which you go up 150 steps to the bell; but it is not allowed to be rung. There is also a striking clock on that tower, which was the first and last we saw in Turkey; for the Turks have no clocks at all, except small striking ones, which are sent them by Christian potentates, and they do not even know how to manage these. Some of them regulate themselves by the sun in the daytime, and by the moon at night; and more especially in the towns they have their talismans, or priests and chaplains, who divide the different parts of the day by certain measures of water, and who, knowing the hour from these, have to call out from time to time, with a loud voice, from high towers built of a circular shape close to the churches, and summon the people to divine service. They call or scream on the towers for the first time when day is about to dawn; next, instead of ringing bells, they summon the people to their churches in the middle of the space between sunrise and noon; thirdly, at noon; fourthly, at vesper-time; and they call the people together for the last time at sunset, using for that purpose a loud voice with all their might and main, and stopping their own ears. Living in peace and leading an idle life, as they do at Constantinople, they are summoned to prayers seven times a day by talismans or priests, although none but courtiers, unoccupied persons, and persons of high rank, and also merchants, are in duty bound to attend them. Artizans are not obliged to pray more than five times a day, if they do not wish it. Whoever cannot pray in a church, prays, when he pleases, at home, at work in the fields, or wherever the cry of the priest reaches him. Their priests, when they thus summon the people to prayers, scream out like ox-drivers with us, and their voice is heard much farther than one would suppose. Next day we went into the town again, and looked over it. As we returned to the boats we saw the Italian renegade, who had turned Turk, being conducted with a grand procession by the Turks into the town, in the following manner. First went about 300 Turkish soldiers, or azais, with long muskets, who shouted for joy, and some of whom fired; after these rode some horse-soldiers, apparently their commanders; next, five banner-bearers with red banners; after these went some disagreeable gipsy music, consisting of shawms, fiddles, and lutes; next rode the unhappy Italian renegade, on a handsomely caparisoned horse, on each side of whom rode a Turk of rank, and he in the midst, wearing a scarlet pelisse lined with foxskins, and a Turkish cap with several cranes' feathers in it. In his hand he held an arrow, and had one finger directed upwards, thereby making profession of the Turkish religion. After him rode several trumpeters, blowing their trumpets without intermission, who were followed by about 300 Turkish hussars, ornamentally dressed in pelisses of spotted lynxskin, who sometimes shouted, sometimes sprang from their horses, and exhibited tokens of great exultation. When they rode in at the gate, they halted in the gateway, and all thrice made profession of their faith with great clamour, saying, "Allaha, illasa, Muhamet resulach!" *i. e.* "One true God, save him no other God, and Mahomet his chief prophet!" They also fired thrice. They then

c

rode in the same order past our boats, shouting all the time, no doubt in despite of us.

Our chiaous, a German, born at Augsburg, who had renegaded some years ago, told us that the pasha had presented the Italian with a handsome horse, and promised to give him pay to the amount of twenty aspers a day; but it is incredible that he should have given orders to give him so much, for the chief janissaries do not receive so large a sum as pay; and others told us that, when the year was out, he would be in want of bread.   But the chiaous told us this, perhaps, in order to persuade some one else to fall away to the Turks; but, thanks be to the Lord God, this did not happen.

After dinner we went to see the castle of Buda. When we came to the first gate, some soldiers on guard were standing by it, passing through whom we entered a handsome square, on both sides of which there stood cannons, thirty in number, and on the ground lay twenty more without wheels.   Amongst the thirty were some so large that a man could get inside them. The Turks informed us that these cannons had been brought to Buda after the battle of Syget.   From this square we went through a second gate into a second square, and from this through a third gate into a third square.   In this third square is a beautiful cistern made of bell-metal, and eight pipes fixed up above it, through which the water flows into the cistern; but just then it was not flowing.   There is German writing, with an ancient inscription inside the cistern, and the Austrian arms, *i.e.* five larks, four serpents, cray-fish, and other animals, cast in a masterly manner.   Thence we went up a winding staircase into a handsome and spacious gallery, and thence into a circular room, which in the time of King Mathias had been a chapel. Out of this chapel you go into another room, in which King Mathias Corvinus had his library, where the ecliptic is painted with the planets, and two astronomers facing each other. Underneath this couplet is written:—

"Cum rex Mathias suscepit sceptra Boëmæ
Gentis, erat similis lucida forma poli."

"When King Mathias took Bohemia's crown,
This was the form the radiant skies did own."

Next to the library was the royal chamber, in which the kings of Hungary used to live. It is very handsomely painted, and hung with fine tapestry along the sides, where stands a kind of throne, covered with an awning of handsome carpets, under which the pasha sits and holds his council when he comes to the castle. We then descended below, and ascended again by a wooden staircase into a tower, the dungeons in which are very deep and well secured, and in which, at that time, as the Turks told us, there were as many as seventy Christian captives, who cannot escape from it in any way except by the aid of Divine Providence itself, or by paying an enormous sum of money and ransoming themselves. Round this tower are bastions, which strengthen it exceedingly, and on it stand three cannons on wheels, one of them a piece cast by the Bishop of Gran. We afterwards went to a large palace, in which there was nothing particular to see. Lastly, returning down the Danube, we crossed to the city of

Pesth, opposite Buda, by a bridge 600 paces long, constructed of large boats. In this city there are both
Christian and Turkish merchants, but the buildings are
poor. We saw nothing handsome in it, and therefore
returned to our boats. That day a courier from Vienna
overtook us at Buda.

On the 13th of October the pasha summoned my
lord the ambassador and the courier into his presence,
and sent his own boat for him, into which the ambassador got, with six persons, and went to the pasha.
After settling his affairs our lord went into Buda himself, and our chaplain performed mass in a Christian
church. After dinner we started from Buda; the
pasha assigning us his kapigi pasha to supply us with
provisions, and also four chiaouses to conduct us safely
to Constantinople, and four janissaries for protection.
The chiaouses perform the duty of commissaries, or
ambassadors, and execute every command given by the
Emperor or a pasha; and this office is very honourable in the eyes of that nation. They assigned us, also,
six large boats, in which those chiaouses voyaged, fast-
ening our boats to theirs. A provision boat also sailed
after us, in which a number of poor captive Christians
were being taken to Constantinople for sale, with whom,
however, the Turks did not allow us to speak. On this
night, for the first time, we reposed on pretty tolerable
beds in the boats.

On Oct. 14 we started early from the bank, leaving
a large village, called Sadum,* on the right of the
Danube; and here we saw the first inn, which they call
a caravanserai. This was all covered with a leaden

* Szegedin.

roof, like all their inns. At noon we stopped at some vineyards and dined; at even we sailed to a village called Little Paksha, lying on the right of the Danube, and there spent the night.

On Oct. 15 we sailed past Great Paksha, which is a very handsome little town on the right of the Danube, and in which is a handsome caravanserai, or inn, and two Christian churches. At noon, as it was no longer so dangerous, we lashed all our boats together and dined, sailing on without intermission as far as Belgrade; * therefore I shall not now write any more the names of the places where we dined. Towards evening we sailed up to a town called Tolna, which is the last Hungarian town, and in which, up to the present time, the greatest part of the population has been Christian, dwelling under the protection of the Turks, and possessing a church of their own, a Calvinistic minister, and a school for youth. We here procured very good wine, and filled our bottles.

On Oct. 16 we sailed on during noontide, dining on the boats; at the hour of vespers we stopped off a town called Seremian,† where there is also a Christian church, but all forsaken and almost ruined; however, Christians do perform their devotions in it. And here we passed the night.

On Oct. 17 we came again to a beautiful champaign country, and sailed on amidst delicious meadows on both sides of the Danube. During this part of the journey we also saw a great many swans, geese, cranes, storks, and ducks, some of which we shot and ob-

---

* White castle.   † Sirmien.

tained.   The whole of that day we passed through
most beautiful meadows; at night we arrived at a
village called Perykmart,* and took up our quarters
for the night.

On Oct. 18 we did not start till about ten o'clock in
the morning, and that because one of our boats, on
which the horses and carriages were, as it started from
the bank, stuck in the sand, and could not be moved;
three Turkish boats hastened to its assistance, and were
obliged to drag it by force out of the sand.   Here we
spent the night again in excellent beds.

On Oct. 19, with morning dawn, we sailed to the
place where the river Drave falls into the Danube, half
a mile above Erded;† we also, afterwards, sailed past
Erded.   It is a castle on a hill, on the right of the
Danube, and beneath it is a tolerably large village.
At the hour of vespers we arrived at Walpowar, and
stopped there about an hour.   It is a pretty little town
under a castle, and that a handsomely built castle.
Close to the town is a wooden bridge, that the Turks
may be able to go dryshod into the country when the
Danube is flooded.   Here we furnished ourselves with
good provisions and wine.   Towards evening we
passed the village Sodin, on the right of the Danube,
near which we saw a large ruined castle, and spent the
night in beds not far from that village.

On Oct. 20 we sailed past Moshtin. ‡   This is a
ruined castle on a hill, and a village under the castle,

---

* Pringwart.   † Erdody.

‡ The German translator says that this and the following day's
journal describe circumstances entirely different from those exist-
ing two centuries later.

lying on the right bank of the Danube, containing a
Christian church. We then sailed by Illoi, a delightful, cheerful little town, by which there is a castle on a
hill, on the right side of the Danube. A bishop's see
was here in former years. After that we passed a village called Panestra, lying on the right of the Danube,
by which there is a fine ruined castle   Then we sailed
by Skerveta, a town on a hill with a castle in it. At
nightfall we sailed to Petrowar, otherwise called Peter-
wardein. This is a castle on a hill, enclosed all round
by a high wall, and under the castle a clean little town,
where we spent the night, and purchased some provisions
and wine.

On Oct. 21 we sailed past Carlovitz, which lies on
the right of the Danube. This is a large town, in which
are two Christian churches of the Greek religion, and a
third which is Catholic. On the left side of the Danube
we saw Tytel, a handsome town, as they informed us,
above which stands a castle on an eminence. We afterwards sailed by Selemek, which is on a lofty hill; but
now nothing remains but ruined walls and some old
towers, which have not fallen down from the rain.
Close to the ruined castle is a town surrounded by a
wall, and embellished by numerous towers, some of
which are already in ruins. Opposite this town, on the
left hand, the river Tisa* falls into the Danube after
flowing through Transylvania and Hungary.

On Oct. 22 we started early, leaving the town of
Semen on the right of the Danube; immediately afterwards we espied Belgrade,† on the side on which the

---

* Theiss.   † White castle.

rivers Drave and Tisa* fall into the Danube. Belgrade
lies on the side and at the place where the river Swinie,
or Sava, meets the Danube. Here, on the last corner of
the promontory as it were, stands the old town, built in
the ancient style, with a good many towers, and surrounded by two walls, and the rivers of which I have
just mentioned flow up to it on two sides. On the side
on which the land is continuous it has a strong castle,
upon a tolerably lofty eminence, with many lofty towers
built of hewn stone. In front of the city are numerous
houses and a large suburb, in which live people of various nationalities, as Turks, Greeks, Jews, Hungarians,
Dalmatians, Transylvanians, and others. Indeed, in
nearly all Turkish districts the suburbs are always
larger than the cities ; and both at once exhibit the
appearance of large cities. In this town there is nothing particular to see, only the bazaar, in which the
merchants keep their wares, is covered with a lead roof,
and built square ; round and round, below it, are vaulted
cellars for the security of the merchants' goods, and
inside, above, galleries run round with rooms and shops
everywhere. In the middle of this building is a handsome square and a large cistern, into which water flows
through a large round stone like an aqueduct, on
which is engraved: *"Qui crediderit et baptizatus fuerit
salvus erit. Anno* 1538." "He who believes and is
baptized shall be saved." There is also in this city a
special house, in which Christian captives are sold. The
Christian merchants have no church there, but the

---

* This is not correct, as the Drave and Theiss fall into the
Danube on opposite sides.

Catholics perform their worship in a house, and maintain a priest at their own expense.

They would not let us all go into the castle; but we saw many pieces of ordnance standing on the walls. At last, through favour and through presents made by my lord the ambassador, I and his cousin and one chiaous were let into the castle; but they would not show us anything particular. We saw, however, that it is a well-fortified fortress, and could not be taken very easily. Within the recollection of our grandfathers this city and castle were attacked by the Turks with undoubtedly a powerful force, first by Sultan Amurath, and afterwards by Mahomet his son, who took Constantinople; but because at that time the Hungarians and crusaders defended themselves valiantly, both enterprises of the barbarous nations were in vain. Finally, Sultan Soliman, in the year 1520, immediately after the commencement of his reign, besieged it with a large army, and firstly, through the carelessness of King Lewis, then a youth, and secondly, through the disunion and discord of the Hungarian lords, who were disgracefully quarrelling amongst and conspiring against each other, this town and fortress, being unprovided with soldiers and eventually quite deserted, was subjugated by Soliman with scarcely any trouble or difficulty. By this way afterwards, as through an open gate, all the evil rushed into Hungary, by which that nation is now overwhelmed. Through that entrance, as it were, the Hungarian King Lewis was conquered* and lost his life. In like manner Buda, the metropolis, was taken, the land of Transylvania subjugated, Ostrehom and other for-

* In the battle of Mohacz.

tresses taken; a formerly most glorious kingdom is
suffering violence ; the surrounding nations are fainting
with excessive terror; and we poor Bohemians experienced at those times much misery and trouble
through wars in Hungary; a countless sum of money
has been taken out of the country ; a countless number
of people of note and of our dear Bohemian friends
have fallen and been slain in Hungary,—sacrifices of
which the land of Hungary is in no wise worthy. And,
unless the Lord God pleases to aid us specially by His
divine assistance, it is to be expected that these our
deadly foes will force their way into Austria, and at
last into our own beloved country,—which may the Most
High mercifully forefend! Moreover, hitherto there
has been no real love and unity amongst us; the
worthy and upright Bohemians and fathers of their
country have perished, and if there be any, there are
very few remaining : but the majority consists of such
as would be glad that foreign nations should invade
these countries, and destroy this our famous Bohemian
kingdom. But I have already digressed far; I will return again to Belgrade.

On Oct. 24, before we moved from Belgrade, a dispute arose between my lord the ambassador and the
kapigi pasha assigned to us. It being his duty to
supply us properly with provisions, he neglected to do
so, supplied us badly enough, and kept the money for
himself. My lord the ambassador wished, therefore,
to send a courier on horseback to Buda, and lay a complaint against him before the pasha; but the kapigi,
conscious of guilt, and being a cunning fellow in such
matters, contrived to prevent our obtaining any such

courier for any sum that we offered. My lord the ambassador was, therefore, very angry with him, and threatened that, if he did not immediately supply us with better provisions, he would complain of him at the court of the Turkish emperor. The kapigi, fearing this, promised to set all to rights, and supply us with provisions with which we should be well contented.

On Oct. 27, after preparing in this city everything necessary for the journey by land, our Vienna coach-men started in good time with the horses and carriages out of the boats, and we seated ourselves in the car-riages, and travelled, without intermission, by land from Belgrade to Constantinople. The same day, leaving on the left hand the castle of Smederow on the banks of the Danube, which had formerly been the abode of the despot of Servia, we arrived at our first stopping place for the night, Isanlak, or Little Palanka, a miserable village, and passed the night there.

On Oct. 28 there met us on the road a new court-official belonging to the pasha of Buda, called by the Turks a *defterdar*, whose office it is to take charge of his lord's money, and lay it out for necessaries, accord-ing to his order. Beside him rode some Turks on horse-back, and behind him five pages, who carried his lances and shields. Some camels and mules followed, and a carriage containing his wives. In the evening we arrived at Great Palanka, and then for the first time spent the night in a Turkish inn, by the side of our horses; for in the more simple inns they have no other rooms.

Here it seems to me requisite to give some account of these inns or caravanserais, which we made use of on this journey, and which are most peculiar to Turkey.

Such an inn is a large building, somewhat broader
than long; in the midst it has a wide level space, in
which the guests place all their baggage, and put up
their camels and mules. Round this space is a wall
about three feet high, reaching to the walls, which
contain the whole building, and constructed like a kind
of bench. This wall is, moreover, level, and four feet
wide; on it the Turks have their beds, their kitchens,
and their eating-rooms; for, as has been related, the
whole building is contained by walls. Here are constructed fire-places with chimneys, at which the guests
prepare their food; neither do they separate themselves
from their camels, mules, and horses, by anything more
than the space of the wall, although they tether their
horses so close to it, that those animals can stretch their
heads and necks over it and stand like servants before
their masters, or act as such, when they are playing or
supping. Not having any troughs, these ·animals eat
their fodder out of knapsacks, and stand so close by
their masters that they can now and then take a piece
of bread, an apple, or anything else out of their hands.
On this wall the travellers arrange their beds as follows :
first they spread a carpet, which they carry with them
for the purpose, fastened on a horse; upon this they
place their *talaman*, or mantle, and instead of a pillow
put a saddle under their heads : they then cover themselves for the night with a long, lined pelisse, (in which
they ride and walk,) instead of a feather bed.* Lying
down in this position they sleep so pleasantly that they
have no need of any luxuries. Nothing is secret there,

* An Englishman would have said, coverlet or counterpane.

everything is done openly; no one can do anything apart from the eyes of others, except in the night and darkness.

There are abundance of such inns in Turkey; and because all the Turks that were there stared at us when we ate, and wondered at our customs, our ambassador would not willingly spend the night in them. A further reason was, that no small stench proceeded from both human beings and cattle; and we, therefore, always looked out to procure my lord a night's lodging in some Christian cottage: but these huts were so confined and narrow that there was frequently nowhere to place a bed. When, therefore, my lord the ambassador had been provided for, we, the rest of the company, prepared our night's lodging on rugs and carpets in the carriages, under the carriages, and wherever we could. Sometimes, however, we spent the night in Turkish hospitals, which are handsomely built, covered with a lead roof, and very comfortable for travellers, because a number of empty rooms are found in them, which are shut to no one; but, be he Christian or be he Jew, be he rich or be he a beggar, they are open for the convenience of all alike. The pashas, sangiaks, and other Turkish gentlemen also make use of them, when they travel across the country, and cause this kind of building to be erected for the comfort of travellers. We, too, frequently had a good and quiet night's lodging in them, and slept our sleep out as long as we liked. The following custom is also observed in these hospitals, viz. that the Turks give food to whoever comes there. When the hour of the evening meal comes, each of the superintendents of the hospital brings a tray or broad plate, (in some places

they have tin ones,) with a rim round it two fingers
high, like a moderate-sized round table, on which, in the
middle, stands a dishful of boiled grains of barley, or
sometimes of rice, boiled down to soup, and a tolerably
large piece of mutton. Round the dish are cakes of
nice-looking bread. Sometimes, in addition to this, they
brought a small dish of honey or honey-comb, and begged
us not to despise their food. My lord the ambassador,
certainly, declined, but we of the suite, having healthy
stomachs, accepted it very gratefully from them, and
they brought us a third and even a fourth dish. We
liked it very well, ate it up, and, after thanking them,
gave them an asper or kreutzer as a trinkgeld. They
prepared similar food for all the Turks who travelled
with us. A stranger may make use of this comfortable
provision for three days gratis, but immediately after
that must change his inn. These hospitals have large
endowments and revenues, for the principal and more
religious pashas and Turkish grandees have them built,
assign them revenues, purchase villages for them, in
their lifetime, and after their death leave them no small
sum of ready money. Let this be enough about the
inns and hospitals, and also about the nights' lodgings,
which we made use of on our journey, as opportunity
offered.

On Oct. 29 we arrived at Budesin, which is a simple village, and in it an inn, which is not a very good
one ; and here we found six Christians, who had been
captured by the Turks at Vesprim in Hungary, and
were being taken to the city of Sophia for sale. In
the evening my lord the ambassador summoned the
four chiaouses, or commissaries, and the four janissaries,

and in their presence complained how meanly and improperly he was supplied with food, though no small sum of money for expenses had been given by the pasha of Buda to the kapigi pasha, and, therefore, he was determined not to allow his suite to perish of hunger. Thereupon he had a casket brought and opened in their presence, containing the ready money intended for the Turkish emperor, and took out thence a bag of money, in which were more than 2,300 florins,* and gave notice that he, the ambassador, would spend that money in the purchase of food and other necessaries, keep an account of it, and complain of the kapigi pasha at the Turkish court, and that should the matter in any way come home to him, he must not blame anybody but himself. The chiaouses said nothing in reply, but that the kapigi had orders to provide us with proper food. On that day's journey, though at a great distance, the Turks showed us from the higher ground the mountains of Transylvania, almost at the place in which stood the pillars of the bridge of the Roman Emperor Trajan.

On Oct. 30 we arrived at the village of Jagoden, which is tolerably large and handsome. Immediately as you enter it stands a handsome Turkish mosque, or church, with a lead roof. There is also a spacious caravanserai, where we kept our horses, but we ourselves lay outside of it in a peasant's house, rather than in the stench. Opposite our inn was a second Turkish church, and in front of it a cistern, ornamentally constructed of white marble, in which the Turks, according to their

* The exact sum is 200 meissen kopy, or rouleaux containing 60 pieces of money. Jungman gives each kopa at 11 florins 40 kreutzers, which gives 2,333 florins 20 kreutzers, or £233 6s. 8d.

custom, wash and purify themselves before they go into
the church; for they maintain and believe that, if they
pray without washing, their devotions are of no value.
They also leave their shoes outside in front of the church,
and go in barefoot. It is incredible how they hold to
cleanliness in their churches; they do not suffer any
dirt, cobwebs, or rubbish to be in them, neither do they
allow a Christian to enter them, unless he has obtained
leave by presents. Moreover, they do not permit any
dog or domestic animal to go in. They enter the church
with the following humility and lowliness, after taking
off their shoes. They prostrate themselves silently on
the ground, kiss it, and pray as fervently as if they saw
God there with their own eyes. No one lounges or
walks about in church, no one chatters with another,
and nothing else is heard but fervent prayer. All of
their temples are carpeted on the ground, or covered
all over with matting, on which, according to their
custom, they stand with bare feet, kneel, or sit cross-
legged. No snifting or spitting is to be heard there,
for they consider it a great sin. If it happens to any
one that he has sneezed involuntarily or spit upon the
ground, he immediately goes out of the temple, purifies
himself again, and washes himself with water. Let me
speak briefly. These Pagans are more fervent in their
religion than we Christians, who have the true knowledge of the Lord God Almighty, and ought, therefore,
day and night to give thanks to his Holy Majesty that
we have come to that true knowledge, and be more fervent in our prayers than we are.

On Oct. 31 we were ferried across the river Morava,
not far from Jagoden. This river divides Servia, or

Serbsko, from Bulgaria. The country is very beautiful but desolate, for the Turks do not cultivate much of the plains, and do not willingly practise agriculture, and the Christian peasants are nearly the only people who work in the fields. Having ferried our horses and carriages across the river, we arrived at night at a village called Kasen, which is miserable and in ruins; and, there then being no inn in it, we were obliged to go to rest as we could, some of us in cottages, others in the open air, and others under the carriages.

On Nov. 1 we came to the brook Nyssus, which flowed almost always on our right, till we arrived at the town. Here they reckon it to be half-way between Vienna and Constantinople. When we came to the inn the grooms, unharnessing the horses, rode carelessly with them into the stream, which flows through the town, and is fifty paces wide or more, in order to water and wash them. A servant of Herr Hoffman's fell unexpectedly into a deep place, lost his seat, and shouted for help. A groom, wishing to help him, threw him a horse's halter, which Herr Hoffman's servant clutched so tight that he dragged the groom also from his horse. The horses swam out, but it was impossible to help the men, and they were both drowned. My lord the ambassador gave orders afterwards that they should be sought for, taken out of the water, and buried. On the bank of this stream, in the town, where signs of a Roman road are still found, we saw a lofty marble pillar, with an inscription in Latin letters, but already so damaged and obliterated that they could not be read. Nyssa is a tolerably populous place, and there we rested.

D

On Nov. 3 we came to a small town called Kuric-
hesme, in which there is no inn. On the left hand
flows a stream called the Zukava. On the 4th we
started early, and by vespers saw the town of Pirot,
but, without halting, dined off what we each had on the
carriages. Close to this town, on a height, is a ruined
castle, of which only the walls are standing. In the
evening we arrived at Tambrod, a miserable village
without an inn; and here we spent the night.

On Nov. 5 we spent the night in the village called
Bobitza, and next day arrived at the city of Sophia.
This is tolerably large and populous, and in it resides
the Beglerbeg of Greece. It formerly belonged to the
kings of Hungary, then to the despots, or princes, of
Servia, as long as their dynasty lasted, and till it
perished through the Turkish wars. The beglerbeg
ordered us to be welcomed by his chiaouses. Early in
the morning he sent several handsome horses to our
inn, on which our principal personages mounted; and
my lord the ambassador seated himself on the beglerbeg's own riding-horse, which was a very handsome
one; the saddle, reins, and all the trappings were studded
with precious stones, and certainly cost many thousands.
Mounting these Turkish horses, we rode to the beglerbeg in the same manner as at Buda, and on arriving at
his abode saw on one side about 100 janissaries, on the
other, the same number of spahis standing in a long
row up to his chamber. When we entered the hall we
found it hung round with handsome Persian tapestry.
There sat the beglerbeg on a chair, and my lord the
ambassador also seated himself on a chair opposite to
him. Behind the beglerbeg stood two boys, dressed,

like most beautiful maidens, in gold brocade, with broad girdles set with precious stones. The beglerbeg himself had on his head a large cap, and at the back of it a handsome plume of cranes' feathers. He was a particularly clean-made man, of good stature, of handsome and cheerful aspect, and we had not seen a better-looking Turk upon our journey. According to the Turks' account he was to marry a daughter of the Turkish emperor. When my lord the ambassador presented the letter to him, he received it very reverently, conversed cheerfully with my lord, cut several jokes, and it was immediately apparent that he was a courtier. After this my lord the ambassador delivered to him the presents from his Imperial Majesty, viz. two silver-gilt bottles, after that a large gilt striking-clock, shaped like a Turkish turban, upon which stood a chamois, which turned its eyes backwards and forwards, and when the hour struck pawed with its foot and opened its mouth, and under this gilt serpents and scorpions twisted about.

After our return to the inn, the beglerbeg sent to us, requesting my lord the ambassador to present him, according to former custom, with 200 broad dollars, and asking whether he was inferior to his predecessors. But my lord excused himself, saying that he had at that time no money for him, but only for the Sultan, but the deficiency should be made good for him. The beglerbeg was thus avaricious and greedy of money because he had not long obtained this office, and had been obliged to pay well for it. In this town we stayed in a very handsome and lofty inn, with galleries inside, and clean private apartments; nowhere else during our

journey did we enjoy such comfortable accommodation
in any inn as there.

On Nov. 8 we started from Sophia, leaving the small
town of Bossen on a height on the right. In the evening we saw another small town, Falup, on the right,
and at a well found an old Turk, born at Vienna, who
had been captured and carried off at the siege of Vienna,
and, being unable to withstand the Turkish tyranny,
had turned Turk, and had now almost forgotten the
German language. During this day's journey, as on
we went, we saw cleaner villages and towns, of which
there were as many as seven, than at any other time.
We had a pleasant day's journey; the plains were
beautiful and fertile, and also the Bulgarian vales. In
these localities we ate, for some days in succession,
loaves baked under the ashes, which the Turks call
"fugatia." These loaves are baked and sold by the wives
and daughters of the people, because in these regions
there are no bakers. When, therefore, the women learn
that strangers have arrived, from whom there is a prospect of earning money, they hastily make up meal
with water, and without leaven, put the dough into hot
ashes, and while it is still hot—or, as we say, bread
from the oven—sell it at no great price. Other eatables,
e. g. mutton, fowls, hens, and eggs, are sufficiently
cheap there, and could at that time be bought, for the
present wars had not yet begun. That night we lodged
in the village of Jessiman.

I cannot here forbear mentioning the dress of the
peasant women in this district. They go in white
shirts or smocks, which are of corded linen, not very
thin, and of all colours, embroidered with Turkey yarn

made of plain silk upon the seams, round the hem and
waist, and almost everywhere.   In these they are extremely well satisfied with themselves, and despise our
plain thin shirts.   Their head-dresses are tower-shaped,
very comical, and covered with hats of platted straw and
lined with linen, just as the peasant children with us
make hats of green rushes.   The part which with us is
broad below, and meets the head, they wear wide above,
and top-shaped, in a manner more suitable for catching
the sun and rain than for any other purpose.   These hats
stand about one and a-half or two Prague ells above their
heads.   They have also glass beads round the neck and
in the ears, and ear-rings hanging from the ears to the
shoulders, like a variegated rosary ; and in these they
are just as satisfied with themselves as if they were
queens of Bulgaria, and walk as grandly amongst
strange people.

Of this Bulgarian nation it is related that, when
divers nations changed their abodes, either voluntarily,
or driven from their homes by other nations, it migrated
from the Scythian river, called the Volga, to these parts.
Thus these Bulgarians are so called, *quasi* Vulgarians,
or Vulharians, from the river Volga.   They established
themselves in the mountains called Hæmus, and between the city of Sophia and Philippopolis, in places
naturally strong and defensible, where they lived, and
for a considerable time paid no regard to the power
of the Greek emperors.   They captured in battle and
put to death Baldwin the Elder, count of Flanders, who
ruled the Empire of Constantinople ; but not being able
to withstand and resist the Turkish power, were over-
come, and obliged to endure the miserable and heavy

servitude which they suffer up to this day. They use a Slavonic language, so that we Bohemians can converse with them.*

On Nov. 9 we travelled over mountains without intermission. At noon a chiaous from the beglerbeg caught us up, and brought after us the clock which had been presented to him, as the Turks, not knowing how to manage it, had overwound it and broken a string, which our clockmaker was obliged to put to rights when we stopped for the night. Before we arrived at the plain, which surrounds the city of Philippopolis, we were obliged to travel by a narrow road, over a steep mountain, where there still stands in the midst an ancient stone gateway, called Derwent Kapi, the gate of the narrow way. Here lived the last despot, or prince, of Bulgaria, Mark Karlovitz; but now the whole building is so ruined and desolate that it presents no likeness to a fortress. We spent the night in the village of Janika, without an inn.

On Nov. 10, after starting, we saw the river Hebrus, which takes its rise in Mount Rhodope, not far off, and a handsome stone bridge over the same river, which the Turks call the Maritza. In the evening we arrived at the city of Philippopolis. This city lies on one of three heights, distant, and, as it were, separated, from the other mountains, and which were purposely digni-

* In 1852, I received by post two copies of a Grammar of the Bulgarian language, by A. and D. Cankof. It exhibits every appearance of being a corrupted Slavonic; but there are many non-Slavonic roots in it. In Aug. 1861, I had the pleasure of meeting a Bulgarian gentleman at Prague; but his language was unintelligible to the Bohemians, and *vice versâ*. Our medium of communication was Polish, which he spoke well.

fied by building the town, and placing, as it were, a
beautiful crown upon them. In the suburb is a second
wooden bridge over the river Hebrus, which flows
alongside the city; not far from this we lodged in an
inn, and stayed two days in the city.

On Nov. 12, on starting from Philippopolis, we saw
rice growing like wheat in swampy places. The plain
is full of small hillocks, or mounds, raised above the
ground, like a kind of graves, which the Turks assert
to be barrows thrown up in memory of battles which
took place in those plains. They also believe that these
mounds are the graves of people slain there in battle.
That day we crossed the river Hæmus by a handsome
bridge of hewn stone, and afterwards travelled through
a beautiful wood or forest. Leaving the river on the
left, we spent the night in the village of Papasly,
where there is no inn. At that village a chiaous came
to us from Constantinople, bringing my lord the ambassador a letter from Herr Petsch, who had been there
several years continuously as imperial resident,* and
was now very anxious to be replaced by another ambassador, and return home.

On Nov. 13 we arrived at the village of Usum Sha-
vas, in which there is a well-built inn, with handsome
apartments; and there we spent the night. The next
day we came to Harmandli, a pretty village, where is
a bridge 160 paces long, and a handsome inn, with a
lead roof, where we lay during the night.

On Nov. 15, keeping close to the river Hebrus, which
flowed again on our right, and leaving, on the left, the
mountains of Hæmus, which extend to the Black Sea,

* Orator.

we went over the celebrated stone bridge, called Mustapha Pasha's bridge.   In this bridge there are twenty-
two arches, and the bridge itself is above 404 paces
long.   We next arrived at the village of Shimpry,
where there is a handsome inn, and a Turkish temple;
and we spent the night in that village.

On Nov. 16 we arrived at the city of Adrianople, in
Turkish Ændrene.   This place was called Oresa before
it was enlarged by and named after the Emperor Adrian.
It is situated just where the Hebrus meets its tri-
butaries, the Tunya and the Harda, and thence the
united streams flow together into the Ægean Sea, which
separates Asia from Europe.   The city is not very large
in circumference, but there are extensive suburbs round
it; and it is owing to the buildings constructed by the
Turks that it has grown to its present magnitude and
extent.   Over the river there is a very large stone
bridge.   Here we had an inn of no great excellence,
although there were many others handsomely built;
this being, next to Constantinople, the largest city in
these countries. On Nov. 17 we rested there and looked
over the city, where there is nothing particular to see,
except the inns, and two temples,* very handsomely
built of stone.   These temples are circular inside, and
in them are three galleries, with large pillars, built of
white and red marble, round which are iron rings, at
the bottom of which hang 326 handsome glass lamps.
Higher over these is a second set of rings, from which
ostrich-eggs and balls of looking-glass are suspended by
silken straps.   Over this, again, is a second gallery, all

* I have pretty uniformly translated the word *kostel* by "church,"
and *chram* by "temple."

round which is a set of rings with lamps, and above a
second set of rings with ostrich-eggs and balls of looking-glass. On the third and highest gallery is a set of
iron rings, and lamps all round suspended from them.
Highest of all, in the midst, hangs a gilt ball. All
these galleries are adorned with remarkable marble pillars. In the lowest sits the Turkish emperor, where
there is a kind of alcove. The Turks told us that these
lamps, of which there are over 2,000, burn day and
night, and that they require seventy pounds of olive-oil
a day. In the middle of the church are two handsome
cisterns of white marble, into which water flows through
pipes. Next to them is a pulpit of white marble, into
which no one enters except their highest priest, who
goes up twenty-five marble steps, and reads and ex-
pounds the Alcoran to them. Sultan Selim had this
new church thus ornamentally built at the time when
he wrested the kingdom of Cyprus from the Venetians.
He assigned it large revenues from the resources of
that kingdom, which are transmitted every year to
Adrianople. There are four very high and slender
towers, and in them three galleries, as in a church, one
above the other, from which the priests summon the
people to prayers; and when they hold the annual
festival, called Bairam, lamps are hung out at night
from the towers. From these towers we had a view of the
whole city. In this city there is also a palace belonging
to the Turkish emperor, on that side of the river on
which Sultan Selim dwelt; but they would not allow us
to enter it.

On Nov. 18 we started from Adrianople, and travelled
to Hapsala, a small town, in which is a handsome temple,

an inn, and a hospital, erected and endowed with large
revenues by Mahomet Pasha, in which a dish of rice
or soup and a piece of mutton must be given to every
comer till the third day.

On Nov. 19 we passed through the town of Esky
Baba, in which is a handsome church, and an inn, ornamentally built by Ali Pasha.   Here a beg from Moldavia had taken up his lodging, who had formerly been
a prince there; but having been accused before the Sultan, by another Moldavian prince, of wishing to cause
a disturbance, draw the people from their obedience,
and revolt, he was sent for by the Sultan, who intended
to have him beheaded.   Seeing that there was no escape,
he then turned Turk to save his neck, but only on condition that he was to be reinstated in Moldavia.   This
renegade prince had taken up his quarters with some
thousands of Turks, not only in the town, but also in
the neighbouring district, otherwise we should have
spent the night there.   The other, who had accused
him before the Sultan, hearing that he was to be reinstated in his office, escaped with all his property into
Christendom.   Not being able to stay there the night,
we went to the village of Bulgagium, which is princi-
pally inhabited by Greeks, and spent the night there.

On Nov. 20 we passed through the town of Burgash,
which lies in a plain, and in front of which is a stone
bridge thirty-seven paces long.   Immediately after
leaving Adrianople, whithersoever we went we saw
abundance of flowers, which was to our no small astonishment, because it was the month of November.
In Greece there is an abundance of the sweet-smelling
narcissus and hyacinth, so that through their numbers

they affect the head and brain of a person unaccustomed
to the scent. The Turkish tulip has hardly any scent,
and yet many people value it for its beauty and the
variety of its colours. The Turks are fond of surrounding themselves with flowers, and, though they are
not over-prodigal of their money, still they do not grudge
laying out a few aspers, or kreutzers, for an inconsider-
able flower. Flowers, and presents also, cost my lord
the ambassador, and ourselves, a good deal; for when
the janissaries and other Turks brought them as presents, we were obliged immediately to give an asper or
so in return, and thus show that we were grateful for
the gift.

And, in truth, whoever wishes to dwell amongst the
Turks cannot help himself, but, as soon as he enters
into their territories, must immediately open his purse,
and not shut it till he leaves them again, and must constantly be sowing money as a kind of seed, since for
money he can procure himself favour, love, and everything that he wants. And, if no other advantage comes
therefrom, at any rate this does, that there is no other
means of successfully taming and quieting the Turks,
who are of a ferocious character from their birth, and
different from other nations. The Turks allow themselves to be calmed by money, as by some delightful
strain, otherwise it would be impossible to have any
dealings or transact any business with them. Without
money foreigners would scarcely be able to live amongst
them, or visit those regions, for the Turks are shameless
and immoderate in taking money and presents. Even
pashas and other great lords, when no present is made
them, have the audacity to ask for presents through

their underlings, and sometimes gratefully accept very miserable donations. For instance, one day at Constantinople, when my lord the ambassador wished to have a brief conversation with Synan Pasha, and we were waiting before his apartment, a shepherd, who was an achamolglan, *i. e.* a kidnapped Christian, who had already become a Turk, came into the room amidst ourselves and the Turks, carrying a live sheep on his shoulders, and walked, without intermission, in front of the door, when it was opened for people to go into the pasha, till the pasha noticed him. The pasha immediately ordered him to be admitted, sheep and all, into his presence, thankfully received the sheep, and gave audience to a shepherd in preference to the imperial ambassador. But, to tell the truth, my lord the ambassador had no worse fault than stinginess and unwillingness to spend money, though he knew that love is bought from the Turks by presents ; a thing which afterwards the unhappy man, as well as ourselves, had bitterly to pay for ; an account whereof will be given in the proper place. That day we travelled to Karystra, a simple village without an inn, whence my lord the ambassador sent a horseman to Constantinople, and gave notice of his approach to Petsch, who was there as imperial resident.

On Nov. 21 we came to the town of Churli, or Korlii, a good memorial of the unfortunate war which Sultan Selim waged in those regions with the pasha, his father, when he escaped out of battle by means of his horse Karavulik, *i. e.* black wolf, saved his neck, and took refuge among the Tartars of Perecop, where his father-in-law ruled. After some years, by dint of great promises and gifts, this same Selim obtained the throne, drove his father out, and ordered him to be poisoned in this town, as the Turkish chronicles describe at length. Here, for the first time, we saw the sea, and had it always on the right hand. We spent the night in the town.

On Nov. 22, before we arrived at Selebrya, a town on the sea, we saw manifest tokens of ancient earthworks, or walls, which were constructed from this city to the Danube, by order of the last Greek emperors, in order that the district might be surrounded and enclosed with fortifications, that is, that the villages, lands, and property of the people of Constantinople might be safe from the incursions of foreign and barbarous nations. In Selebrya we were much delighted by the cheerful and pleasant prospect over the calm sea, so that I could not restrain myself from running down with some of the rest, without the leave and knowledge of my lord the ambassador, or his steward, and gazing upon the sea, of which I had never had a glimpse before, till I was satisfied. We ran down to the shore, and wondered at the swimming and leaping of the dolphins and other fish, and I collected some very beautiful striped shells, and forgot to return to the town. Meanwhile, the Turks in the town saw a caicque, or pirate boat, making straight for the shore, with its sails spread. The chiaouses pointed the boat out to my lord the ambassador, and warned him not to allow any of his suite to go far from the town, affirming that the pirates sometimes stayed the night somewhere on the coast, and lay in wait to kidnap people and carry them off. When this prohibition was issued, and not till then, I and my companions were missed. It being ascertained that we had gone to the sea, the chiaouses and janissaries immediately mounted their horses, and, taking their weapons, raised a shout, and galloped to the sea. There they found us admiring the boat, which was still about three hons* from us, and drove us to the town. Upon this the pirates shot about three arrows from a bow at the shore, and a janissary fired his gun at them in return. Here we were welcomed by my lord the ambassador; some of the elder of our party were beaten with a stick, and I was to have a whipping with a horsewhip, because no birch grew in that place. However, I had first a long lecture from my lord, and he was then going to have me whipped, although, conformably to my uncle's orders, I had always endeavoured to conduct myself so faithfully and obediently towards him that he might not have any reason to scold me. I was always ready to perform his wishes, if I did but know them; and day and night I endeavoured to serve and satisfy him above all others, and he was consequently very kind to me. On the present occasion, being dreadfully frightened, I did not know what else to do but humble myself, and promise that, to the day of my death, I would never allow myself to do anything of the kind without his leave and knowledge. The Turks also spoke in my favour, laying it to my youth and folly, so that I was excused the whipping; but, nevertheless, a lecture was read me till my ears tingled. Thus my curiosity and running wild, because I wanted to see the sea before the rest, almost brought me to the point of being captured by those sea-thieves; and had our friends not known of us in good time, God knows whither I

* A hon is 125 paces.

might not have been taken and sold. Here we afterwards spent the night.

On Nov. 23 a courier on horseback again arrived
from Herr Petsch. For our night's lodging we went
to the town of Ponte Grando, where there is a stone
bridge 787 paces long, with twenty arches, over an arm
of the sea.

On Nov. 24 we arrived at the town of Ponte Picolo,
or Little Bridge, for there, too, you must go over a
bridge. These two arms of the sea are very pleasant,
and if they were to be adorned by human aid and
labour, and if human intelligence and cleverness were
to assist their natural features, I do not know that there
would be anything more beautiful under the sun ; now,
however, left, as it were, forlorn, they give tokens how
they bewail and lament their forsaken condition, because,
on account of the servitude whereby they are bound
to a barbarous lord, people hate them, dislike them, and,
finally, take no notice of them. Here we saw fish caught
with large nets in the sea : the fishermen caught a large
number of very good and well-flavoured fish, and sold
us those which we wished, and as many as we wished.
At this town Herr Petsch had ordered his steward to
welcome us, and furnish us with good provisions.

On Nov. 25 we started at three o'clock, and about
ten o'clock saw Doctor Petsch, the resident at Constantinople. He had with him a good many horsemen
both from the Turks and from his own suite, and, in
particular, about forty chiaouses, or courtiers, of the
Turkish emperor had been sent to meet us, who welcomed us, and rode before us into Constantinople.
Here, first of all, when my lords the ambassadors saw

each other, they dismounted from their horses, and embraced each other with great joy, as if they had long known each other. Herr Petsch was more especially delighted, as he was aware that there was something brewing among the Turks before it broke out, and knew that he was to return to Christendom in a few days.

During this day's journey we lost two of our company, the clerk of the kitchen and a Hungarian tailor. These persons, wishing to get to Constantinople before us, left the road and were seized by the Turks, who imprisoned them in one of the emperor's summer-houses, went off, and rode to Constantinople to ask Bostangi Pasha what they were to do with them. Meanwhile the Hungarian tailor broke loose, and helped his companion to break loose from his bonds. Being thus freed from their fetters, they fled and concealed themselves; nor was it till the third day afterwards that they got to us at Constantinople. Moreover, the Turks took from them all the money they had with them, at least thirty ducats, and it is a certainty that, had they not broken loose, they would have been taken and sold somewhere beyond the sea.

This day we went for a long time through the city of Constantinople before we arrived at the hotel assigned to us, which was built of square red stone, and covered in with a lead roof. Immediately as you enter it, through a great gate, is a clean and tolerably spacious square, with gates on each side, and a stone staircase, by which you can ascend to the gallery, which is of stone, and runs all round. Underneath is a kitchen, wine-cellars, and stabling for 200 horses. Above, on the same floor as the gallery, are very comfortable rooms all round, with Italian stoves in them. In these my lord the ambassador took up his abode facing the street, and we were distributed by threes and fours in different apartments, according to our personal dignity and position. Whoever goes to court must go past this house, which is built in so convenient a situation, close to the principal street, that everything can be seen from it.

As regards the situation of the city, it seems to me that the place is prepared by nature for the site of an imperial metropolis. It certainly lies in Europe, but has Asia and Egypt* almost before its eyes, and Africa on the right hand. Though these lands do not adjoin the city, yet they are, as it were, united to it by the sea, and an easy voyage. On the left are the Pontus Euxinus and the Lake Mæotis, or, as the Turks name them, Karantegise, or the Black Sea, beside the waters of which many nations dwell, and into which many rivers flow on all sides. Moreover, there is nothing produced in these regions for the use of man that cannot be easily conveyed in boats to Constantinople. From one side of the city stretches the Propontis, or Sea of St. George ; on another, a harbour for vessels is formed by a river which Strabo, from its shape, called the Golden Horn ; the third side of the city joins the land : so that the city itself has the appearance of a peninsula, and, with its whole elevation, forms a promontory running into the sea, or an arm of the sea.

---

* This is not quite correct ; but in several places the author seems a little at fault in his geography. Perhaps the words " and Egypt " should be omitted.

E

From the midst of Constantinople is a very pleasant and delightful view over the sea, and of Mount Olympus * in Asia, which is constantly white with snow. The sea contains a great abundance of fish, which at one time swim from the Lake Mæotis, or the Black Sea, through the straits of the Bosphorus into the Ægean and Mediterranean, and at another, turn back again, as is the nature of fish, in such immense numbers that abundance of them can be taken by the haul of a very small net. Thus it is that there is such an abundant fishery of divers fish, and that they sell them so cheap. †
The fishermen are usually Greeks, and are also well acquainted with the art of cooking fish. Neither do the Turks despise fish, when they are well cooked, especially those which they consider clean. Still, it is not every natural-born Turk who is fond of them, but rather the renegade, or Christian who has turned Turk. Moreover, frogs, snails, tortoises, oysters, and the like, a born Turk not only will not eat, but will not even touch. In fact, in the Alcoran unclean fish and wine-drinking are alike prohibited to the Turks, and no one in any official position whatsoever drinks wine, except in secret. This is usually done by renegades, who used to come to us in secret, drink for whole nights, return secretly home before dawn, and beg us earnestly to let no one know of it. But the unruly youth and the soldiers do not allow themselves to be kept in order; nay, they go into Christian taverns, eat as much as they please, and pay nothing ; and if the host does not wish to be beaten he

---

* The German translator says, " Olivet !"

† The different fish are enumerated; but their names are not all in Jungmann's Lexicon, so I have thought it best to omit them.

must not say a single word. And, when they get drunk, every Christian or Jew whom they meet gets as far out of their way as he can, otherwise, if you have not a janissary with you, you meet immediately with a box on the ear, or a stab. Such persons, when they commit any misdemeanour, are immediately put into prison, and thrashed with a stick for the crime of drinking wine. But I will now return again to our house.

My lord the ambassador, wishing to have access to, and an audience of, Ferhat, the chief pasha, who was of Albanian extraction, a tall, black, long-toothed, and disagreeable man, was obliged to present him before-hand with the gifts sent by his Imperial Majesty; nor till this was done did my lords the new and old ambassadors, and we with them, ride to Ferhat, in the same fashion as at Buda and Sophia. When we had kissed* his hand, and the hands of all the other pashas present, our ambassador delivered to him the imperial letter, which he received reverently, but the presents much more reverently, viz. 3,000 broad dollars, two silver-gilt jugs, with basins, two large gilt beakers, two others, like large gilt bunches of grapes, two large silver-gilt pails, or cans, two large silver-gilt bottles, a large clock in the form of a gilt horse, on which sat a Turk with an arrow drawn to the head, a square striking-clock, on which two men stood and moved, and, when it struck, opened their mouths, a hexagonal ball, like a buzygan, or Turk-

---

* It is not necessary to suppose that the ambassador himself did this, if it was done literally by any of his suite. " Polibuju var-nostiruku,"—" I kiss your hand," is a common form of politeness in Bohemia from an inferior to a superior. It might probably be translated simply, " saluted."

ish mace, in which was a gilt striking-clock, and so
forth. From Ferhat we afterwards rode to the Vizier
Muhamet, who had been barber to the preceding emperor, and, after kissing his hand, gave him from his
Imperial Majesty 1,000 rix-dollars, an ewer with a silver-
gilt basin, and a large clock in the shape of a sea-horse,
adorned all round with various shells. Having transacted all necessary business with him,—(he was a born
Hungarian, but had turned Turk,)—we returned to our
hotel.

Another day we went to three other pashas, and also
to a chiaous, who was by birth a Croat, and had a
daughter of the Turkish emperor to wife; to Ibrahim
Pasha, who was also a Croat; and to Cykula Pasha, who
was by birth an Italian, from Messina, and at that time
captain, or high admiral. Having saluted these pashas,
we gave them 1,000 dollars a-piece, a silver-gilt jug,
with a basin, a silver-gilt bottle, in the shape of a moon,
two large double-gilt beakers, a clock like a Moor leading an English dog by a chain, and another clock, on
which was a Turk sitting on horseback, and behind him
a lion overpowering another Turk, all which moved
when the clock struck, and the horse pawed with his
foot, and turned his eyes every minute. To other officials simpler presents were delivered by the steward,
dragoman, or interpreter of my lord.

BOOK II.

Of the Residence of the Imperial Embassy at Constantinople.

THESE three pashas, and many others, as well as various Turkish officials, whether captured in childhood, or in manhood, and afterwards converted to the Turkish religion, although the children of Christian parents, and although many of them had lived a considerable time in the Christian faith, are, nevertheless, not over-kindly disposed towards Christians. And it is matter of wonder that they have arrived at such great dignity; for they regulate the whole dominions of the Turkish emperor, containing numerous kingdoms and princedoms, and govern them by their wisdom and understanding, on which depend the whole management of the lands of the Turkish emperor. As long as any one of them lives, so long does he remain in honour; but when he dies, everything—were it millions—falls again into the imperial treasury, for the Emperor says to them:—" Thou hast been my man,* thou hast gained wealth from me; it is a proper thing that, after thy death,

* *Chlap;* Polish, *chlop,* a serf.

it should be returned back again to me." Their children
do not inherit any landed property, unless their father
secretly provides them with ready money, or helps them,
in his lifetime, to some office, or procures for them an
estate, or a current pension from the Emperor. Never,
therefore, did I hear it said of any pasha, or observe,
either in Constantinople, or in the whole land of Turkey,
that any pasha was a natural-born Turk; on the contrary, they are either the kidnapped children of Christian
parents, or persons captured in childhood, or persons who
have turned Turks.

They told us, for instance, that Cykula Pasha was
captured, when twelve years old, in a boat with his
father, and that when the Turks promised him that they
would release his father from captivity provided he
turned Turk, he did so, wishing to aid his father. The
Turks, certainly, did release the father; but sent him
home so carefully that he died within three days. The
son, who had become a Turk, having once tasted Turkish freedom and pleasures, proceeded gradually to worse
and worse, till now he will have nothing to do with
Christianity; but, on the contrary, is pasha and high-
admiral, and is a great enemy of the Christians, as he
showed in the battle of Erlau, in Hungary, in the year
1596. In that battle, when our soldiers had given themselves up to plundering the Turkish tents, he, with his
fifteen renegades, or Christians who had become Turks,
charged back again upon our men, forced them to flee,
and was the cause that so many Bohemians and good
men were slain.

Synan Pasha, (who was at this time *mazul,* that is,
deprived of all his offices, and being, as it were, in dis-

grace with the Emperor, was living on his estates, and
was the person who afterwards had us put into prison,)
and Ferhat Pasha, an audience at whose house I have
mentioned above, were both of an Albanian family,
first cousins, and employed in feeding swine. On being
taken captive they were placed, with many other kidnapped children, in the Emperor's serail, or palace, and
were entrusted to the chief cook to learn cookery ; but
in the case of Synan Pasha something else displayed
itself as regards his future destiny. Watching an opportunity, when the Emperor Selim was about to go
out riding, and having taught himself the Turkish language, he fell on his knees before the Emperor, and
humbly begged him to order him and his cousin to be
taught to read and write, and not to leave them any
longer in the kitchen. The Emperor, looking at his
person, was pleased with his figure, and therefore
immediately gave orders that so it should be. Being
both taken out of the kitchen, in a short time they
learned so successfully to read and write Turkish that
Synan surpassed all the other boys in wit, strength, and
beauty of language. The Emperor, learning this, had
him instructed in riding, running, wrestling, and shooting with the bow; and herein he many times displayed
such distinguished heroism before the Emperor himself,
that the latter, and his courtiers, were struck with admiration, and Synan was made an itzokdan, or page.
On arriving at a maturer age he begged that he might
go to war with some pasha or other; and there he behaved so heroically that he obtained honour and praise
above all men. He was first made an aga, or captain,
and conducted himself so manfully that he was often

the cause of victory. For instance, he did the Christians a great deal of harm at Famagusta, in the island of Cyprus. After this he became beglerbeg, then pasha, and lastly grand vizier. He was also engaged at the siege of Malta, conducted a campaign against the Persians, and remained some years in favour, which continued till a few weeks before we arrived at Constantinople. He was then, no one knows why, suspended from all his offices. However, as a faithful friend, so long as fortune favoured him, he never forgot his cousin Ferhat, but always helped him higher and higher, till, finally, he helped him to the highest dignity, so that Ferhat had, in our time, been made grand vizier, in the place of Synan.

With regard to Ferhat, Herr Resident Petsch related to us, that, some years ago, (at that time Herr Petsch was secretary to the imperial ambassador at Constantinople, and Ferhat a pasha,) the imperial ambassador died, (to the best of my recollection he was an Austrian gentleman, Herr von Zizing,*) and when his corpse had been removed to Austria, the Emperor Rudolf thought fit to appoint and confirm Herr Petsch, seeing that he was a worthy man, as his ambassador in place of the preceding one. It being a custom among courtiers to wish each other joy of their posts, Ferhat gave orders for Herr Petsch to be visited and congratulated on his new office through his steward. The steward informed Herr Petsch that he ought to give the pasha about 1,000 dollars, and a handsome beaker. He sent him the beaker, but no money. When, therefore, Ferhat was made grand vizier he sent for Herr Doctor Petsch,

* Pan z Cycynku.

and asked him, with vehement reproaches, why the
annual present, which they call the tribute, had not
been paid.   Herr Petsch excused himself, and proved
that the time had not yet come, and that no tribute had
ever been in arrear ; nay. he promised that he would
send one of his servants to Vienna, and expressed his
willingness to take measures for the tribute to be brought
earlier.   The vizier, having nothing else against him,
had him asked, through an interpreter, where the King
of Vienna (for this is the appellation they give our emperor, refusing to call him emperor, and asserting that
their Sultan is the Roman emperor, as the throne of the
Roman emperors was transferred from Rome to Constantinople) obtained the power of being able to make
a rascally clerk into so distinguished a resident at the
court of the Turkish emperor ?   To this, Herr Petsch
answered without thinking, that, if the Sultan had the
power to make swineherds and cowherds into the highest
pashas, his lord, the Emperor of Rome, had the power
of making a clerk into an ambassador, and of sending
whom he pleased to the imperial court at Constantinople.   Thereupon Ferhat smiled, and admiring his
audacious language, merely said these words, in Turkish,
to the bystanders : *"Baka, baka, pre haranzada gaur !"*
that is, " See, see this audacious pagan !" Let us now
pass again to our own embassy.
On Dec. 8, early in the morning, my lord ambassador
Kregwitz had the ready money, 45,000 broad dollars,
placed in carriages, and sent it beforehand to the imperial palace, with his dragoman, or interpreter.   Then,
about ten o'clock, both my lords the ambassadors rode,
after the previous fashion, to the Emperor with their at-

purpose, who immediately collect and clear it away.
They afterwards dry the horsedung in the sun, beat it
with a mallet through fine sieves, and make it into
litter for the horses; for no straw can be obtained for
litter in Constantinople. Our people also learned this
from the Turks, and littered the horses in this way, and
when the horses had become used to it they rested as
willingly upon it as upon straw.

When we had dismounted, my lords the ambassadors
went on foot through the gate into the third square, and
we after them. Two pashas, counsellors of the Sultan,
came out to meet and welcome them. At this gate
stood several hundred janissaries. The two pashas led
my lords the ambassadors into the divan or council, and
we stood there also; and upon its being explained to
the pashas what was to be said to the Sultan in conversation, they gave orders that nothing else should be said
but what they had now heard. The two pashas went
first, with their hands placed crosswise, out of the council-
chamber, and proceeded to the Emperor to announce my
lord the ambassador. This third square is large and
clean, and the imperial apartments are opposite the gate.
On both sides and also on the third side, where the gate
is, the whole building is only two stories high; the
eunuch chamberlains live in the apartments on the right
hand, and the Emperor's wives in those on the left. From
the gate to the imperial apartments stood about two or
three thousand janissaries on the right, in caps and
coloured mantles, that looked as if they had been painted,
and on the left as many spahis or horse-soldiers, who
were, however, on foot, there being no horses there,
quite up to the imperial apartments. And although

there were some thousands of people there, nevertheless there was no shouting, no conversation, no moving hither and thither, but all stood so quietly that we could not help wondering; nay, even the janissaries, although furious and licentious people in war, here observed greater obedience towards their commander than boys towards their preceptor, standing as quiet as if they had been hewn out of marble. The aforesaid two pashas, when they came walking, without any suite, between these spahis and janissaries, laid both hands on their breasts, and bending their heads, did obeisance first to the janissaries and then to the spahis, all of whom, by way of reply, bent their heads almost to their knees, and stood thus stooping till the pashas had passed them all. And when the pashas had announced the imperial ambassadors, saying that they desired to kiss the Sultan's hand, they again saluted the spahis and janissaries on both sides, returned to our lords the ambassadors, and instructed them how they and the principal persons of their suite were to behave in the Sultan's presence. They also forbad my lord the ambassador to take any number of people with him; and he acted on their advice, not taking with him any but persons of baronial or equestrian rank. The presents of silver plate were held by janissaries in front of the Emperor's apartment, that he might see them.

My lords the ambassadors, and we in their train, walked after the pashas through these troops, and did reverence to all of them on each side, taking off our hats and bending our heads, which was done to us in return by them. When we arrived at the imperial apartments, an eunuch, Kapi Aga, the chief chamberlain, came out

to meet us, who, after doing obeisance and welcoming
us, conducted us into the great saloon or hall, which
was all hung with valuable Persian tapestry and carpets
interwoven with gold and silver. Here again the pashas
went once more through one room to the Sultan, and on
returning asked our lord whether he had any weapon,
dagger, or knife about his person. Both my lords the
ambassadors having answered that they had nothing of
the sort, the two pashas took them each by one hand,—
a custom observed among the Turks ever since a Croat,
having requested and obtained an audience, assassinated
Sultan Murad, and avenged the death of his lord, Marko,
the despot of Servia. The chamberlains opened a door,
concealed by handsome tapestry, glittering with gold
and precious stones; and these pashas conducted my
lord the ambassador into the presence of the Emperor,
and made a low obeisance to the Emperor. My lord
the ambassador made as though he would kneel upon
his knees; but the pashas, by order of the Sultan, held
him up, and did not allow him to kneel upon the ground.
Then a dragoman or Turkish interpreter, a renegade, or
Christian who had turned Turk, was brought, and spoke
in short sentences to the Sultan, at the dictation of my
lord the ambassador.

First, he delivered the greeting from his Imperial Majesty, and then kissed and presented, with an obeisance,
his letter credential to the Sultan, which the Sultan
handed to Muhamet Pasha, as his chancellor, and asked
how our Emperor was in health. After these questions
my lord the ambassador stood aside. Thereupon, in the
same manner and form, Herr Petsch was introduced by
the two pashas, kissed the Sultan's hand, and also stood

aside. After that, having all been previously searched by the Turkish chamberlains, to see whether anybody had a dagger or knife—but, of course, knowing that we should be introduced to the Emperor, we had nothing of the sort—we were conducted, one by one, by the chamberlains to the Emperor in the same room, and, when each had kissed his hand, were again conducted out of it. I cannot describe the apartment where the Emperor sat, on a place about half-an-ell elevated from the ground, and covered behind him with very beautiful gold brocade cushions, embroidered with precious stones and pearls, for it was impossible to notice it in so short a time, and, indeed, I looked more at the face of the Emperor than at the beauty of the room; only there were some balls hanging from the ceiling, which glittered very much, but I do not know whether they were made of looking-glass, or studded with precious stones.

After transacting our business, we returned from the divan in the same fashion, and the pashas invited my lords the residents to take refreshment, and placed a table for them in a separate room, where they dined sitting on chairs, although the Turks are not accustomed to eating at a table, and sitting on chairs. They entertained us, also, in the open saloon, but on the ground, which was spread with handsome carpets. But, before they gave us anything to eat, we saw how the Turkish emperor is served. First came about 200 cup-bearers, or servers, dressed almost uniformly in red silk dresses, and with caps on their heads like those of the janissaries, except that about a span above the head they were embroidered with gold. These having placed themselves in a row from the kitchen to the Sultan's apartment,

first did fitting reverence to all by an inclination of the
head, and then stood close to each other, just as if they
had been painted figures. When it was dinner time,
the superintendent of the kitchen brought from the
cook a porcelain dish, and another covered dish, handed
it to the waiter nearest him, he to a third, and so on till
it came to the one who stood nearest to the Emperor's
apartment. There, again, stood other chamberlains,
and one handed it to another, till the viands were carried very quickly, and without the slightest noise or
clatter, to the Emperor's table. Several of them again
placed themselves in a similar row to the place where
the pashas and my lords the ambassadors were ready to
eat, and handed the dishes from one to another till they
placed them on the table. About sixteen of them, also,
placed the viands in the same manner upon the floor,
which was covered with carpets, first covering the carpets with handsomely-embroidered Persian leather, instead of table-cloths. Our viands were boiled and baked
fowls, soup and rice, sweet mince-meat, baked mutton,
and salads of small, and, to us, unusual and disagreeable
herbs; we had painted spoons, no knives, and no wine.
When any one wished to drink, a Turk, who had at his
girdle a vessel of Persian leather, distended like bagpipes,
with silver-gilt trumpets attached to it, poured out into
silver-gilt goblets a sweet-water compound of sugar and
lemons, which they call Arab sherbet, and handed it to
the guests. This water I like very well.

Having spent here about half-an-hour at dinner, we
rose from table, and some janissaries, having received
from us the presents intended for the Emperor, took
them away to their quarters. These presents were as

follows:—a large silver-gilt ewer, with a basin; a second basin, silver-gilt, with handsome twisted and chased work, with an ewer; two large cans, like water-cans, ornamented with pomegranates and flowers, silver-gilt, and ornamented with enamel; two large silver-gilt goblets, in the shape of a Turkish cap; two large silver-gilt pails, all with work of masterly workmanship; two large silver-gilt candlesticks; also, two pair of gilt snuffers; two large gilt dishes, a large gilt bottle, in the shape of a moon; a hexagonal ball, artistically adorned with chains, which twisted themselves surprisingly when the clock struck; a clock in the shape of a tower, upon the striking of which, Turkish jugglers, in the different rooms, ran about and peeped out; another striking-clock of chased work; a large square clock, a master-piece of art, upon the striking whereof Turks ran out, mounted on horses and fought, and, when it left off striking, went in again; a long clock, on which stood a wolf, carrying a goose in his mouth, on the striking of which, the wolf fled, and a Turk hastened after him with his gun ready to shoot, and when the last stroke was about to strike, shot at the wolf; a large square smooth clock, on the top of which a Turk turned his eyes, and when it struck, moved his head and mouth. After dinner we returned to our hotel in the same fashion in which we had ridden to the Emperor.

List of the Persons who came with my Lord the Ambassa-dor to Constantinople.

Herr Frederic Kregwitz, ambassador of the Roman Emperor, Rudolf II; Andrew Hoffman, George von Landau, Kregwitz, the brother of my lord the ambassador; Albert von Thurn, Frederic Malowetz, Gebhard Weltzer, John Frederic von Oberheim, Kaspar von Hohenfürth, Henry Schwenitz, Smil Zahradetzky, Francis Jurkowitz, Conrad Pretorius, the physician; John Pertholdt, John Seltzer, John Kapl von Turkhaus, William Wratsky, John Reinhart von Stampach, George Reitter, Ladislaw Mörthen, the steward, (who afterwards turned Turk;) Bernard Schahner, grand equerry; John von Winorz, the chaplain; Gabriel Hahu, the secretary; John Rhandleberger, the vice-secretary; my lord's gentlemen, Eustace von Prankh, George Lasota; the chamberlains, Adam Wolfgang, John Malowekz, Mark Reindler; pages of the chamber, Sigismund Fink, Melchior Kregwitz, John Perlinger, John Wenzel Wratislaw von Mitrowitz, Stephen Lang, Balthazar von Kopet; Kasper Malek, the interpreter, or speaker; Paul Gertzemond, the cup-bearer; Luke Meminger, the purveyor; Henry Jahn, the caterer; Sebastian Hausnik, the cellarer; Frederic Seydl, the apothecary; Christopher Haas, the barber; Blasius Cyrenthaller, the goldsmith and clockmaker; John Æder, the silversmith; Michael Fisher, the painter; Christopher Warazda, the Hungarian tailor; Daniel Ragsky, the sacristan; the chief-cook, Christopher N.; the remaining cooks, John Tyngel, Philip Peckstein, Jacob Brenk; the confectioner, Wawrinetz Schmid; the grooms, John Halpach, Isaac Czoth, John Pockh; Kilian Shenkel, the blacksmith; Christopher Zikan, my lord's coachman; John Bornamissa, Peter Weber, Janush Krabat, John Reich. These were the attendants of my lord the ambassador, besides the rest of the suite, who came with the carriages, and returned back again with Herr Petsch to Vienna.

F

When we returned to our hotel, we each got our rooms ready for ourselves, as the attendants of Herr Petsch vacated them for us, and prepared for their journey from Constantinople to Vienna. After living with us here about a fortnight, Herr Petsch took leave of the pashas, and, bidding adieu to us, left the city with great joy, for he had already, to a certain extent, perceived that some change would take place.

After the departure of Herr Petsch, our ambassador gave a splendid entertainment every day, and whoever of the chief Christians and Turks thought fit, might dine with him, so that scarcely any day passed without our having Turkish guests, in whose company we saw many of their customs, and asked questions about the rest. There was also assigned to us, for guard and safety, that no one might injure us, or enter into the house without the leave and knowledge of my lord, a chief chiaous from the imperial court, an old veteran, whom our lord had to keep in food daily, pay monthly wages to, and clothe twice a year. The chiaous had three servants, who never went out all at once. He being lodged on the ground-floor, close to the door of our house, and his attendants above him, they all gave attentive heed to the persons who went hither and thither, and never let any one into the house whom they did not like. There were also assigned to this chiaous, for our protection, whenever we wished to ride or walk anywhere in the city or out of the city, four chief janissaries, for whom a fixed quantity of food, monthly wages, and two suits of clothes a year, with silver trumpets and staves, had to be provided by my lord the ambassador. Orders were also strictly given them by their aga, or captain, to take care that no harm happened to any of us. The Turkish sultan gave orders to provide and deliver to us provisions daily, viz. a quarter of an ox, two sheep, six fowls, a certain measure of rice, sugar, and honey ; forage for the horses, spices, salt, raisins, and wine; and a Turk, whom they call a saka, brought us water for necessary uses in leathern bags. To this man, also, my lord the ambassador gave food and annual wages. Not having anything else to do, we learnt music, of the kind each liked, and some of us learnt the art of shooting with bows and arrows.

Once upon a time some of us being curious to see the church of St. Sophia, we took a janissary with us in order to see it. We were admitted to it through special favour and indulgence, and also through presents and the intercession of the janissary, and saw it throughout. It was erected by Justinian, the thirteenth eastern emperor, and he continued building it at great expense for many years in succession; but the Turks have now made it into their own mosque, or conventicle.   It is a circular and very lofty building, in the form of the Roman temple called the Pantheon, which Agrippa built, and which is now called the Rotunda; but the church of St. Sophia is much higher and wider.   It has in the midst a very lofty vaulted roof, and a circular crypt, into which light enters merely by an opening made to let in the air.   It has three very handsome galleries, one above the other, adorned with remarkable marble pillars, of wonderful height, and so thick that two men can scarcely embrace one of them ; there are, also, many lamps constantly burning in it ; in a word, I never saw a more beautiful temple.   It is said that, in the time of the Christians, this church was much larger, and more extensive by many appendages; but these have long gone to ruin, and only the choir itself, and the middle part have remained. Almost all the Turkish temples are built upon the model of this. In this temple there is still a picture of the most Holy Trinity in the ceiling, near the imperial seat, formed of good mosaic work of various colours, which the Turks leave in its original form; but they have put out the eyes of all the persons, and Sultan Selim shot an arrow at this picture, and pierced the hand of one Person, and the arrow still sticks in it.

Close to this temple are the tombs of the Turkish emperors, and of some of their wives and children, who have been strangled. These are of a circular form, like a kind of chapel, and covered with a lead roof. Each sultan's, or sultana's, coffin is wrapped in valuable and beautiful scarlet, and covered at the top with gold brocade. At the head of each coffin is a turban, made of very beautiful and fine linen, which they wore on their heads while living, as well as a very beautiful bunch of cranes' feathers. Behind the head of each coffin stand two large wax-candles, on candlesticks, in the form of round and pointed balls, which, however, were not at that time lighted. By the side of the coffin of the Turkish Emperor Soliman was a beautiful sabre, adorned with precious stones, and a bow and a quiver, in token that he had ended his life in war. In these chapels, where the dead bodies lie, are constantly, day and night, talismanlars and hodzyaslars, Turkish monks, appointed for the purpose, who, sitting cross-legged, after the Turkish fashion, say prayers for the dead bodies, and sing mournful hymns.   It is impossible not to admire the masterly manner in which this temple, and the sepulchral chapels round it, are built. Whichever way you go to the temple, there are open squares, with a very handsome marble cistern in each, in which the Turks purify themselves after their fashion, before they enter the temple.   We saw not only this temple, but, by means of fees, almost all their conventicles, which are adorned with beautiful marble columns, and are certainly objects of great admiration to a person previously unacquainted with them.

The same day we also saw their imarets, or hospitals, and also their baths, and bathed in them.   It is true that the Turks do not spend much money on buildings, nevertheless, the principal people lay out large sums on mosques, baths, hospitals, and inns, and have them built in an astonishingly handsome style.   As regards the remaining houses, we lounged as much as we liked up and down the city, but sought in vain for beauty in either the buildings or the streets, the latter of which, by their narrowness, put an end to all agreeable appearance.   Amongst the historical reliques there is the wide site of the ancient Hippodrome, or measured space for horse-racing, in which you see two copper serpents. There is also a stone column, square and wide below, and pointed at top, and two other columns worthy of mention ; one opposite the caravanserai, or hotel, where we lodged, and the other in the market-place, which they call the Auratpasar, or woman-market.   On this column, from bottom to top, is engraved the history of the campaign of the Emperor Arcadius, who had it erected, and his own statue placed on the top.   This

column may rather be called a winding staircase than
a column, on account of the steps constructed in it,
upon which you can ascend inside from the bottom to the
top.   This column, which stands opposite the house of
the ambassador of our Emperor, without reckoning the
pedestal or basement, and without reckoning the capital,
is formed of eight entire blocks of red marble, so artistically united that it seems to be but a single stone ;
and, indeed, the common people imagine it to be such :
for where one stone is joined to another, the suture is
entwined with a laurel-wreath, and thus the juncture of
these eight blocks is concealed from the eyes of people
looking at the column from below, the whole of it being
ornamented with a laurel-wreath from bottom to top.
This column has clefts and rents from frequent earthquakes, and is fastened together with many iron clamps
and rings, to keep it from falling, and is, as it were, be-
girt with them.   Upon this pillar, as they relate, stood
formerly a statue of Apollo, afterwards, one of the
Emperor Constantine, and finally, one of the Emperor
Theodosius the Elder.   But, owing to the height of the
column, violent winds, or earthquakes, have swept all
these statues away.

    We saw also, in Constantinople, wild beasts of various
nature and form ; lynxes and wild cats, leopards, bears,
and lions, so tame and domesticated, that they are led
up and down the city by chains and ropes.   We saw
also divers reptiles which we had never seen before;
various birds ; all sorts of juggling games with asses,
horses, mules, and other animals, which take place every
day on the open space of the hippodrome, which the
Turks call Almayden.   Here are fencers ; here they

shoot with bows; here are a singular kind of wrestlers naked, except that they wear oiled-leather breeches, that no one may be easily able to grasp and hold them; here they give challenges for wrestling-matches, and wrestle together, and amuse any one who offers them a few aspers.

Here, too, we saw Turkish religious feeling. A Christian, a poor Greek, brought to the place a number of thistle-finches in a cage, and a Turk went up to him and bought them; next, taking out one, he looked strangely up and down around him, and muttered something, and then, placing the bird on the palm of his hand, cried out, *Allaha*, and let it go; and thus he did with the rest also, having no other thought than that he was doing great honour to God and Mahomet, and might expect a certain recompence for freeing the birds from confinement. I also saw green birds there so cleverly trained that they are lured from a great distance, and if anybody holds up his hand, they fly on it, and if he has an asper in his hand, the bird takes it with his beak and carries it to his master, who gives it in return a grain or seed, and puts it back again into the cage; he repeats the same process with each bird, letting them out one after the other. One Turk had, at least, fifteen of these birds, to which we gave away and wasted a good many aspers. Hence it is manifest that in Turkey, as well as with us, knaves cheat the people out of their money by idle tricks. In this open space, as long as peace lasted between our Emperor and the Sultan, every Friday, which the Turks hallow as a Sunday, provided it was fine weather, there met about 800 or 900 young men, Turks belonging to the court, each dressed as handsomely as possible, wearing a long velvet or scarlet dress, and long trousers, drawn together at the ancles, with handsome sabres, bridles, and saddles, and, above all, exceedingly beautiful horses. These they rode, or had led by leading-reins, and each carried in his hand a long stick, as thick as a stout man's thumb, and a fathom and a-half long, like a dart, and had a small wooden hook at his saddle-bow. When they had all assembled, they divided into two parties, and, as with us a game is played among boys on foot, so they rode out against each other on horseback, threw their sticks at each other, and if any one heedlessly rode out too far, they took him prisoner, and set him on one side. When each had thrown his stick, they picked them up from the ground with their wooden hooks, sometimes at full gallop, while others showed their agility by springing down from their horses, and leaping into the saddle without help, and without making any use of their stirrups. Others again, when three or four had hurled their wands at some one, seizing in their hands, at full gallop, sometimes one and sometimes two of them, and, turning in a moment, chased again those who had chased them, and threw their sticks with good aim at their backs. They practise this stick-throwing in order, in time of war, to be able to throw darts sharply against the enemy. And their great agility is certainly matter of admiration, for, as ladies from win-dows, and thousands of the common people are looking at them, each seeks to display his manhood, and show his agility. Here you can see the most beautiful horses, neatly covered with Persian carpets, as the grooms of almost all pashas, begs, and other honourable lords,

ride to that spot with their principal horses, leading
them by ten, fifteen, or more, by leading-reins, and
when one horse is tired, the youths who ride the races
mount another, till all are wearied. Among these youths
was a merry, pleasant fellow, who was courting the wife
—others said the daughter—of a certain pasha. He
had six most exquisitely beautiful horses, so that nothing
could be more beautiful, and everything upon them was
of gold and precious stones; and he was so swift that
no one could get the better of him in a race, for he
sprang down from his horse as though he flew, and
taking up his wand, got into the saddle, as though he
had never been on the ground, chasing the rest just like
a bird, and darting away from them again, so that no
one could catch him : besides, he was so quick in seizing
the wands, and changing them from one hand to the
other, that his agility is scarcely credible; and he, therefore, obtained praise from all. Next to him was a Moor,
or Arab, the chamberlain of a pasha, who also exhibited
great quickness, but was, nevertheless, not equal to the
first, neither had he such swift horses. When they
had played for about two or three hours, tired their
horses, and galloped till they were satisfied, a kind of
penalty was laid upon those who had lost, and a *mahra-
man, i. e.* a handkerchief embroidered with gold, or a
bow and arrows, or something else, was given by the
maidens* to him who had behaved best. This is a far
different knightly amusement to what there is with us;
for when we meet as good friends, we do nothing but

---

* How the maidens gave the prize does not appear, though the
German translator introduces into his text a full account of the
presents showered by fair hands from latticed windows.

challenge each other immoderately in drinking and gor-
mandizing, and make each other eat more than is proper,
and if any one gets drunk and falls downstairs, we are
delighted at having put him in this condition, and laugh
at him.   Moreover, if one refuses to fill his glass along
with the rest, we immediately begin quarrelling, using
compulsion, bullying, and other disorderly proceedings
against the law of the Lord God, whence, afterwards.
arise law-suits and disturbances.   But enough now of
this; may the Lord God himself amend us!

We were also admitted, in company with the janissary, into the stables of the Turkish emperor, and
gazed with pleasure upon his exceedingly beautiful
horses.   These stables are of several kinds; in some are
the principal horses for the Sultan himself, in others,
trotting and ambling horses, mules for carriages, drome-
daries, as well as entire colts, &c. which are brought
every year from Barbary and Arabia for the Emperor.
These have a mane and tail devoid of hair, and are then
like stags.   At the proper time they are put into open
yards to be fed up, and are anointed with a certain salve
to encourage their growth, after which they grow
a very beautiful and slender tail.   The Turks do not
use their horses for riding before four years old, and
they can stand so much the more work, because they do
not exhaust and knock them up so much in their youth
as we do in Bohemia.   We went, afterwards, into the
Emperor's pleasure or summer house, and also into his
garden, but that could only be done at certain hours,
lest anybody should be there.   Here we saw most delightful spots, many kinds of flowers, most pleasant par-
terres and lawns, delightful vales, flowing streams, and

abundance of groves, not so much artificially constructed by men, as growing spontaneously by nature. Here goddesses formerly dwelt; here the muses had their seats; here learned men selected spots for meditation in private. Thus, after gazing on everything thoroughly, and gathering nosegays of sweet-scented flowers, we sincerely lamented that this most beautiful spot, and the whole of this most delightful region, should remain in the power of the Turks. Furthermore, we saw the serail of the janissaries, where they live, and keep themselves in a very tidy condition, possessing guns, sabres, and battle-axes, beautifully polished, and hung up in cloth cases and sheaths. In this place the *atchamoglans* are instructed in all manner of military matters. The serail is not far from the first mosque which Sultan Mahomet caused to be erected, in honour of the taking of the city, on the place where the Christian church of the holy Apostles Peter and Paul had previously stood.

In Constantinople there are also large gardens, surrounded with walls, on which cats usually jump and assemble, waiting at certain hours for people to come and give them alms. For it is customary among the Turks to boil and bake paunches, lights, livers, and pieces of meat, and carry them in wooden buckets up and down the city, crying out, " *Kedy et, kedy et!* " *i. e.* " Cat's meat!" A kitchen-boy also carries on his shoulders a number of spits, upon which are baked pieces of meat, liver, and spleen, and cries in the streets, " *Tiupek et, tiupek et!* " *i. e.* " Dog's meat!" till they ring again. Behind him run three-score dogs or more, looking to him to be served. The Turks buy this food, distribute it to the dogs, and throw it to the cats upon the wall; for

these superstitious and barbarous people imagine that
they obtain especial favour in the eyes of God by giving alms even to irrational cattle, cats, dogs, fish, birds,
and other live creatures; and, therefore, they consider
it a great sin to kill and destroy captured birds, and
prefer to ransom them with money, and release them into
their previous state of freedom, that they may fly away.
They also throw bread to fishes in the water for them
to live upon. They have a custom of distributing
bread, meat, and other victuals to cats and dogs, of
which a very large number are found daily in the
streets, at certain places, and definite times; and it is
an undoubted truth that on the walls of these gardens
the cats breakfast in good time in the morning, and assemble for the second time at the hour of the evening
meal, in large bodies out of the whole city, and stand on the
look out; for we went purposely to these walls, listened
to their caterwauling, and, with great laughter, watched
how they ran out of the houses and assembled. So,
too, we several times saw Turkish matrons and old
women buying pieces of meat on the spit from the
kitchen-boys, or from the public kitchens, which are not
far from this place, and handing them on a long stick
or wand to the cats as they sit on the walls, muttering
meanwhile a kind of Turkish prayers. Pieces of raw
meat are also carried about the city on spits, which the
Turks buy and throw up to the kites, which fly about
in crowds, and catch them in their claws. We, too,
bought some of this meat for fun, and threw it to the
kites, and watched, with great merriment, how they
tumbled over one another as they flew to seize the meat.
A countless number of these kites fly over the city,

and the Turks allow no one to shoot or injure them, saying that it is a sacred bird, because, in the time of Mahomet their prophet, when he began to build a temple in the midst of Mecca, these kites brought him things that were not at hand in sufficient abundance for the building, e. g. sand, stones, lime, and water, and loyally assisted their Mahomet in building the temple. It is in the same city, Mecca, that the body of their false prophet lies very magnificently entombed.

There are, also, in Constantinople certain persons who, for the sake of a Divine recompence, carry everywhere about the city fresh spring water in leathern bags, with tubes in them like bagpipes, out of which they pour the water into tin cups, and whosoever wishes to drink, be he Turk, Christian, or Jew, they give him to drink. Many in their last wills give directions for this, and appoint perpetual wages for persons who serve in this manner.

A great many fowls go also about the city, one after another in a row, and sometimes by tens, twenties, and even fifties, and their guide, who leads them from one house to another, and asks for alms, is either afflicted with defective sight, or blind of one eye. To these no one ever refuses alms, for they hold them for holy people, because they are said to have been at the city of Mecca, and to have visited and seen the most holy tomb of Mahomet. On this account, therefore, desiring nothing for themselves in this world, and not wishing to gaze any longer on vanities, they voluntarily heat an iron red hot, and, strewing a certain powder upon it, hold their eyes over it until they are dissolved, firmly believing that, in recompence for this their blindness, they will be first in favour with Mahomet, and able to obtain an easy access to him for other Turks.

The common Turks have also a very large number of superstitions, and, amongst other things, we observed that, when a Turk saw a piece of paper on the ground, he immediately took it up with reverence, and thrust it into a crevice, just as with us, when a piece of bread lies on the ground, many people kiss it and place it on one side that it may not be trodden upon. When we asked the reason of this honour paid to the paper, our janissaries told us that it was because the name of God was written upon it; and they firmly believe that at the last judgment, when Mahomet summons the Mussulmans, his followers, to heaven out of the places where they are enduring punishments for the sins they have committed here, in order to make them partakers of eternal felicity, it is impossible to get to him by any other way but over a large red-hot iron grating, over which each must go with bare feet. Here, it is said, a great miracle will take place; for every piece of paper which has thus been preserved by their instrumentality will suddenly betake itself thither, spread itself under their feet, and prevent them from feeling any harm or pain from the heated iron. The janissaries, therefore, considered it most wicked in us when they saw how the whole suite used paper for the most odious and contemptible want, and begged us to beware of doing so. Neither do the Turks permit even a rose to lie on the ground, because, as formerly the ancient pagans said that the rose came into existence through Venus, so these superstitious people have allowed themselves to be persuaded and believe that the rose grew from the sweat of Mahomet. But I will now stop, that I may not busy myself overmuch with such empty nonsense.

When we had seen everything in the city, some of the *attachés* obtained leave to sail across the arm of the sea to the city of Galata, which is for the most part inhabited by Christian merchants, Greeks, Italians, and others of divers nations. The ambassadors of the French and English kings, the Venetian, Ragusan, and other ambassadors, have also their hotels in that city. I, too, not wishing to be last, asked leave along with the rest, and my lord the legatus ordered them to take care of me, as I was the youngest of all, for youth is there in great danger. As we sailed across the strait we saw various fish swimming about; and when we arrived at the town, with two janissaries in attendance upon us, we entered the house of a certain *Hanslong*, a German goldsmith, who had settled there, and was employed, as a tradesman, by the sultanas. This person gladly welcomed us, and saw our arrival with pleasure. He had a Greek cook, a very handsome person, who was his concubine. For, without a certain permission and payment, a man may not maintain any woman openly, and take her for wife. Nay, in order for permission to be given him to marry, after the Turkish form, he must make application before the cadi, or judge, and pay well for it. In obtaining such a permission the following custom is observed:— the person who desires to take a wife comes with her before the judge, declares his name and hers, and must declare before him what he is willing to give her as alimony, should he divorce her, and what furniture and goods she brings to him; all which the cadi orders to be

entered in a book. Should he be unwilling to cohabit
with her any longer, he pays her the alimony, and re-
stores her goods, and she must depart. She may then
take another husband, and he another wife. If they
have had children, the husband is bound to maintain and
provide for them. The goldsmith sent to market immediately for all kinds of excellent sea-fish, and ordered
her to prepare us good viands. He had another woman,
too, in his house, who also acted as cook. These two
women prepared for us, in a short time, a remarkably
good dish from oysters, long-heads, round-heads, and all
kinds of exceedingly well-tasted sea-frogs, and also gave
us abundance of lemons, pomegranates, oranges, and
salads, for everything of the sort can be bought as cheap
there as plain apples with us. Above everything else, he
gave us a remarkably good red Greek wine, and, indeed,
treated us so well that all of us, janissaries and all, got
tipsy with the wine. At first I would not drink it; but
at last, hearing such commendations of it, everybody
saying that never in their lives had they drunk better
wine, I, too, allowed myself to be persuaded, inquisitive
boy that I was, and drank with great relish two goblets,
about half-a-pint, though afterwards I felt the effects of
it, as a dog does those of fat bacon. When the proper time came we bade adieu to our friendly host, and
thanked him, begging him to visit our house in return,
and started upon the sea. As soon as I got into the
boat, my head whirled round with me in such a manner,
that I did not know where I had placed myself. In the
first place the strong wine got into my head, and in the
second the wind disturbed it still more, so that when
we got out on the shore the janissaries were obliged to

lead me through narrow streets, where there were few people, for I could not even stand on my feet. And as no one could go into our house without being seen by everybody, my lord the ambassador was at a window and saw me led along tipsy, was exceedingly angry, and wished to have me punished immediately. Seeing, however, that I was quite unconscious, he put it off till the morning, and severely reproved his gentlemen-in-waiting for not taking better care of me. They excused me by saying that I had only drunk a single goblet of wine.

Awaking in the morning before it was day, I was informed by my companions of my good behaviour, and also of the anger of my lord the legatus. So I got up in great terror, put everything in order in my lord's apartments, attended diligently to my duties, in hopes of obtaining favour in my lord's eyes, and also begged the gentlemen-in-waiting for their intercession. When he was going to get up and rang his bell, I ran to him at once, before the rest, fell at his feet, and begged for pardon for the fault I had committed. But he, in great anger, explained to me how I had been entrusted to him by my relatives, in order that he might take good care of me; that on the present occasion, after asking for leave to see the city of Galata, I had so unworthily and thoughtlessly got intoxicated, that the Turks could not but have pleasure, and he sorrow and anger at it. He also explained to me in what danger I had been, and how that, had it not been for the Divine protection itself, young as I was, those janissaries might have led me away and sold me, and how he should have afterwards had to be grievously responsible for me. He added, that, before I had begun life in the world, I had learnt

G

to get intoxicated, and that God would punish him if he were willing to overlook my fault and forgive me. It was, therefore, necessary, as an example to the rest, that I should be duly punished.

He immediately, thereupon, sent for the steward, with whom I had unfortunately quarrelled about a week before, and ordered him to give me fifty good stripes with a leather whip. I kissed his feet and begged him to excuse me, or diminish the number of stripes. The steward might have interceded for me, but he aggravated my lord the resident's anger still more by saying, that, if such young sweet-tooths were to be borne with, they would do it still more. However, the secretary entreated, and obtained, that only forty stripes should be given me. My companions were obliged, in my lord's presence, to prepare and hoist me up, and the steward gave me the forty stripes with interest, and took his revenge upon me. After this I streamed with blood, and was compelled to keep my bed for about a fortnight, on learning which, afterwards, my lord the ambassador was sorry that I had had so much pain, and told the rest that it might have been stopped at twenty stripes. That wine, in consequence, so stuck in my throat that all those years I used wine very sparingly, and immediately afterwards would not drink it at all, though I gladly received Turkish sherbet.

Once, in order to visit some islands in the neighbourhood of Constantinople, my lord the legatus took a boat and made an excursion down the straits to the sea, which the Turks call *Karadengis*, or *Kara Denysy*, *i. e.* Black Sea. This gulf, called *Pontus*, is let by a narrow neck or not very broad passage into the Thracian Bosphorus, twists with many windings round promontories, reaches Constantinople in a day's voyage, and then runs into the Propontis by almost similar straits. In the midst of this place, where it flows into the Bosphorus, stands a large stone with a column, on the base of which a Roman's name is inscribed in Latin letters. Not far off, on the European bank, stands a high tower, in which a light shines at night for the benefit of voyagers, which is commonly called a *pharos*. Not far from this place a small stream falls into the sea, in which chalcedonies and sardonyxes are collected. A few miles from this place they showed us a narrow sea over which Darius, the Persian king, transported his armies against the European Scythians. But almost in the midst between these two sea-passes, or gulfs,* stand two castles, one in Europe, and the other, directly opposite, in Asia. The latter the Turks had already in their power before the taking of Constantinople; the former, where we lived in the Black Tower more than two years in grievous imprisonment, of which I shall give an account below, was erected by Sultan Mahomet not very long before he besieged Constantinople. He caused apartments, handsomely floored with marble, to be constructed in that tower, and dwelt there till he took Constantinople. The Turks use these fortresses instead of a prison for more important prisoners, as I, unhappy youth that I was, was compelled miserably to experience. This prison is well-beset with guards, who live

---

* It is amusing to observe the difficulty which an inland Bohemian has in expressing marine technicalities. He here uses a metaphor from a defile between two mountains to express straits in the sea, which he above calls a "neck."

in a town surrounding the fortress, and twenty-four of them are constantly employed in watching the prisoners in turn, day and night, never go to war, and are as free from duties as the men belonging to the fortress of Karlstein. This is the case in order that they may have nothing to do but watch the fortress and prisoners; a duty which they perform diligently. Therefore, save by the working of Divine Providence itself, no man ever comes out thereof to the day of his death, neither is it recorded that any one ever made his way out of that tower, except in our time, of which I will give an account in its proper place.

Afterwards, we made excursions whenever we liked to those beautiful Greek and Turkish gardens, enjoyed all manner of amusements, and were able to obtain for money all that the heart desired. We got oysters and all kinds of shells out of the sea for ourselves, shot water-birds and various other fowls, on these islands, and also conies, of which there are abundance in one of the islands, and were as happy as kings, without any want, for about a year, so that we did not wish to go home, but longed that we might enjoy so merry, care-free a life to the day of our death.

It once happened in Galata, the city opposite Constantinople, that the son of one of the principal Greek merchants, a well-grown and well-favoured young man, wished to marry. He fell in love with the daughter of another Greek merchant, a very beautiful maiden of about sixteen years old, negotiated with her parents and friends, obtained a favourable answer, and the day was named for the wedding festivity. In order to be the better able to honour his friends, he prepared to sail

himself to the island of Candy for a superior class of
sweet wines; and having bid adieu to his parents, and
taken an affectionate farewell of his bride, started off
tranquilly by sea. The Greek Christians being about
to celebrate a festival, their women went to their baths
to bathe, and amongst them went the bride. Here we
must bear in mind that all the Turkish women, whenever they go out in the street, are entirely shrouded,
except that they have a black kerchief, or veil, about
two fingers wide, before their eyes, so that they can
recognize everybody, but no one can recognize them.
But, though the Christian Greek women are dressed in
the same manner as the Turkish women, yet they do not
shroud their faces, but only wear a thin kerchief over
the head, and everybody can look them in the face.

Well, this beautiful and unfortunate bride, going with
the rest to the bath, and not dreaming of any approaching misfortune, not only did not veil her face, but, like a
young girl, stared in all directions. Just then one of
the principal chiaouses unexpectedly came riding from
the imperial court, with a large suite of servants, to his
gardens, of which he possessed several by the sea
side. Seeing the bride, he, with great excitement, ad-
mired her beauty, and cried out at the top of his voice:
" *Hai, hai, preruzel kisi; hai, hai!*"   " O, the most
beautiful and lovely maiden!" Springing from his horse,
he gave her his hand, and asked her whither she was
going, and whose daughter she was. She, seeing so
dignified and old a Turk,—for he was about eighty
years old,—was frightened, fled amongst the other women, and gave him no answer; but the other women
told him respectfully that they were going to the bath,

that she was a bride, and whose daughter she was.
He then, to be the better able to gaze at her, immediately cried out that he wished to accompany her, which
they could not prevent him from doing. He walked all
the way at her side, and was the more inflamed with
uncontrollable love the further he accompanied her.
After accompanying her to the bath, he squeezed her
hand and said:—"*Allah, sakla, sebibenum dzanum!*"
" God protect thee, my soul!" and mounting his horse,
went his way.

Next day, as soon as morning came, that grey-haired
old Turk rode to the maiden's father, and earnestly entreated him to give him his daughter in marriage, promising that he would provide her with a good dower,
and be a friend to her parents. Her father was greatly
terrified at this request, and told him, as was the fact,
that she was already betrothed, and the day named for the
wedding, humbly begging him not to take it ill, and saying, that, being a simple man, he was not worthy to be
connected with so distinguished a lord, and give him his
daughter in marriage. The Turk, on hearing this excuse, said:—" But her boundless loveliness deserves to
be loved not only by me, but by the Emperor himself;
wherefore, I entreat thee, give me thy daughter!"
When then the father continued to excuse himself by
saying that he had already given her to another, and
that, according to the Christian custom, it could not be
otherwise, the Turk was enraged, and said:—" Well,
I will know whether it can be otherwise or not." Having
uttered this threat, he went immediately to the imperial
court, obtained leave to marry a Christian, and gave in-
stant orders to put the father and mother of the bride in

prison, and secure the damsel herself with a good guard in her own house. He then invited his friends, and prepared a marriage-feast, and sent a number of Turkish women to her at her home with splendid clothes and female ornaments, who laid so many good reasons before her that they at last persuaded her to consent to be his. Her father and mother were then released from prison.

There is this custom among the Turkish women. When any young man wishes to marry, he must marry rather through the information of his female friends than through the observation of his own eyes; for they tell him where a lovely, handsome, and wealthy virgin is to be found, and he may not see her, or even go to the house of her father and converse with her openly; in fact, if he looks in her face before she is his, the Turks used to consider it a sin of the first magnitude. But this is already obsolete with them; for our janissaries told us that no Turkish maiden puts up with the rule that she is not to show herself to her lover, or speak with him, and if she cannot do it openly, she, at any rate, does it secretly. They have, usually, gardens beside their houses, and in them elevated galleries, on which the women dry their clothes and veils; and if a maiden has not such a convenience at home, she goes to the house of a female friend, and having an understanding with her lover, or with his female friends, makes known when and where he is to be in attendance. She goes to one of these galleries, dressed like a goddess, and assiduously dries some clothes, sings with a loud voice, and acts as though she knew nothing about him. If, however, she ascertains that she has proved attractive to the young

man, she neglects nothing that can tend to inflame love.
If she pleases him, negotiations are carried on about
her with her parents and friends, and should they be
willing to give her to him, a certain day is appointed,
when he declares the amount of the dower with which
he endows her, and gives her various presents, and
she, too, must say how much she brings him.   All
these things are inscribed in a book before the cadi, or
judge.

When the wedding-day comes, the bridegroom previously sends a number of camels and mules, in proportion to the wealth of the bride, for her moveables and
goods.   All that she brings him is placed upon them,
and carried to his house, covered with handsome carpets,
and, should the families be wealthy, in red chests.
When all is ready the bridegroom provides a wedding-
feast, or breakfast, for his friends of the male sex in
some other house, and for the women in his own, or
that of his father.   After breakfast the bridegroom
and his friends mount their horses, the women seat
themselves in carriages, and a handsome, gay-coloured,
ambling jennet is sent for the bride, the mane of which
is plaited with gold; this is furnished with a handsome
saddle, and the requisite caparisons, to the utmost of
the bridegroom's means, and is led by a young man,
while four others bear a handsomely embroidered canopy
—the richer people employ none but eunuchs for this
purpose—and a splendid procession is formed to fetch
the bride.   The bridegroom comes with trumpeters,
drummers, and other music, to the bride's house, dis-
mounts from his horse, and enters the house among
the guests.   Then, after a little confectionary has been

eaten, and some sherbet drunk, the bride's father takes her right hand, places it in that of the bridegroom, and bids him to be kind to her. Upon this the four young men hasten up, a fifth brings the jennet, the trumpeters blow their trumpets, the music plays, and the bride seats herself astride on the saddle; the one walks beside her leading the horse, and the four bear the canopy over her. Her nurse, or the female servant for whom she entertains most affection, rides on a horse after her, but no one leads her horse, or bears a canopy over her. Very large wax candles, like altar-tapers, adorned with divers beautiful flowers, gilt and painted, six in number, more or less, are also carried before the bride. The bridegroom rides with his male friends and those of the bride in front, the bride in the midst, and the women in a line behind her, with great joy and triumph, and making their horses curvet merrily to the bridegroom's house. On arriving there he assists her from her horse, leaves her with his female friends, and rides away again among his male friends.

Well, when the above-mentioned chiaous came with a great number of his male friends on horseback, and female friends in carriages, to the Christian's house to fetch his bride, everything was done splendidly, according to the custom above-mentioned. Mules carried presents of clothes in red leather trunks covered with carpets, and the lady was conducted under a canopy from her father's house to his on a beautiful horse, white as snow, with abundance of music of different kinds, and with very large tapers. It was said then that she had turned Mahometan, and that, therefore, the chiaous, having other wives, had immediately assigned her a separate house to live in, had given her many female slaves, and was keeping her in grand state.

Meanwhile the poor Christian bridegroom bought his wines and returned home with joy, without having the slightest idea of what had become of his bride in his absence. When he approached Constantinople the sad and sorrowful news was broken to him that his bride was already disposed of; at which he was exceedingly heart-stricken, and with great weeping bewailed his treacherous misfortune, above all things lamenting that she had married a Turk, accepted the Mahometan faith, and lost her soul. On his return to the city of Galata, her father and mother made known to him with tears what had become of her, and how it had happened, and proved by witnesses that they had been constrained to do as they had done, and compelled to give her to the chiaous. She, too, on learning that her lover had returned home, wrote him immediately a sorrowful letter, bewailing her great misfortune in having been obliged to take another, contrary to her own and her parents' wishes, and begging him touchingly not to be angry with her. He wrote to her an answer, and this was the purport of his letter:—" Since thou hast forgotten thy soul and become a Turk, I know nothing else to say thereto save to bewail thy loss, and finally, as far as I possibly can, to remove thee from my memory, although this comes hard to me, since I have loved thee above all things in the world."

In answer to this she sent him another letter:— " Although I am supposed to be a Mahometan, yet I remain a Christian in heart, as I was before, and perform my customary devotions." She also begged him not to

forget her, and named a day on which he could come to
her in a garden, that she might meet him, relate orally
herself what had happened, and how it had all happened,
and gaze upon him as her lost lover, assuring him, lest
he should be afraid, that she would manage it so well
that he need not fear any danger. The poor young man
allowed himself to be persuaded, and was found on the
appointed day at the destined place alone. The lady
did not long delay coming into the garden, and having
first had a green tent pitched, dismissed all her maids to
walk where they liked, keeping with her a single faithful *confidante*. When her former lover came into the
tent, she told him all with tears, and begged him not to
take it ill, promising to provide him with money and
everything in her power, and never to forget him.

Such secret meetings on their part lasted half-a-year;
but fortune, who is never constant, grudged them
their happiness. He, receiving pecuniary assistance
from her, used to go about splendidly dressed, to the
admiration of all beholders, for he was well-made, and
tall of stature, and being about twenty-four years old,
boasted such beauty that nowhere in the country was
a handsomer young man to be found. He was also
strong in wrestling, and so good in leaping and running
that his equal was not easily found; and he was, therefore, beloved not only by the Christian, but also by the
Turkish youth. Having several times acted carelessly
on these expeditions, he was seen by some one as he
entered the chiaous's garden. This being made known
confidentially to the chiaous, he, as became a wealthy
dignitary, promised to give large presents to the person
who should give him information when the Christian

was in the garden; and, as everything can be obtained there for money, he found no small number of spies, who watched for the Christian day and night, until, one or two hours before evening, they espied him entering the garden.

When this was made known to the chiaous, hearing of his strength and speed, and also knowing that both Turks and Christians loved him, he dared not have him arrested in the daytime. He, therefore, beset the places by which the young man had to return, and which he could not avoid, with stout fellows; and as he returned home, fearing nothing, he was seized and put in prison. The chiaous also had his beautiful wife well watched that night, and in the morning laid a complaint before the cadi, or judge, alleging that she had committed adultery with a Christian, and requiring that both should be sentenced according to law. He also made the matter known to the Emperor and pashas himself, bewailed his fate, and demanded their judgment, adding, in aggravation of the charge against them, that they had been taken in the act. Still, however, many people making intercession for them, the matter was deferred for more than a week. But as the chiaous had previously loved his wife exceedingly, even so, on the contrary, did he now exceedingly hate her, and refused to allow himself to be softened by any entreaties, but caused the mufti, or chief priest, to confirm the sentence of death against them both.

As soon as it became generally known that two such handsome people were to be led to death a countless multitude assembled, and the execution took place in the following order. First rode the sub-pasha, or imperial judge, after him other councillors, judges, and officials, with a guard of janissaries, and with heralds and other officers of justice. Upon this the young man was led out of prison with his hands bound behind his back, and an iron ring on his neck, through which a chain was passed, while two executioners, well-made fellows, in handsome clothes, (for such people are in no odium with the Turks,) held him by the chain on each side; the guard of janissaries went in front and rear, and a countless number of people on horses and in carriages looked on. When the young Greek was led out of prison a great cry arose from both men and women, that it would be a great shame to destroy such a youth, and all compassionated and advised him to become a Turk, promising that they would petition the Emperor himself to grant him his life. He, however, briefly refused to agree to their proposal, and become a Turk. The chiaous pasha, as he was led past his palace, seeing how handsome he was, sent a message to him, saying that, if he would become a Mahometan, he would contrive that he should save his life, and that the beautiful lady should become his wife; but the young man did not allow himself to be moved, but answered that he was sprung from Christian parents, had been baptized and brought up as a Christian, and would also die as a Christian.

They therefore led out the lady, also, from another prison, and placed her on a mule, round which walked a great number of veiled women; she herself was not veiled, but had her beautiful hair plaited in long plaits on both sides, in the Turkish fashion, with one plait hanging on her back behind. She wore a red carmine dress, and had very beautiful pearls round her neck and in her ears, and was certainly a very lovely woman. She wept so piteously that all had great compassion upon her. When the executioners brought her in front of the serail of the chiaous pasha, and related the offer which the pasha had made, she begged the executioners to lead her nearer the Greek, her former lover, on seeing whom she for a long time could not speak for weeping. When, after long wailing, she was able to call him by name, she begged him in Greek, with all her heart, for God's sake, to take pity upon the youth of both of them, and to become a Mahometan, saying that they could then live together many years in joy and happiness. What the woman said to the man during that time was related to us afterwards by Greeks who heard her speak. She spoke to him to almost the following effect :—" Alas ! have pity ! have pity upon me, unhappy damsel that I am ! and remember that we were to have been married, had not a cruel misfortune interfered with it. Cursed be the hour in which I went to that bath ! My life and death are now in thy hands ; harden not thy heart, I beseech thee ; grant the wish of the great pasha. Have pity upon ourselves, our parents, and our friends, and be not so hard-hearted, being able to help us both, as to neglect it. Nay, rather let the sun and moon beam still upon us whilst we are young. Say—alas ! I entreat with the most earnest entreaty possible—that thou art willing to become a Mahometan." In answer to all these words he briefly answered her that she should rather entrust her soul to the Lord God, and not speak in vain.

The Turks, on hearing this, gnashed their teeth at

him with great anger, crying out,—"*Hai, hai! pre-gaar gidy Tuipek, gidy anaseny, sigligum iste mes sentu kazdyny?*" — "Ah! utterly accused traitor, dog, why refusest thou that beautiful lady?" And thus, with great clamour and tumult, they led him to execution, she, also, riding after him on the mule, weeping from her heart, while the Turks, and Turkish women, comforted and encouraged her. When they had conducted him beyond the *Unkapy*, (*i. e.* beyond the sand-gate,) under the wooden gallows itself, to which were suspended six large hooks, two executioners with their sleeves tucked up fixed the pulleys by which they intended to hoist him up. They then stripped him of his coat and all his clothes, leaving him only his linen trousers, tied his hands and feet, and drew him up towards the gallows upon these pulleys higher than a man's height.

Just at this moment the lady rode out from the gate, which is not far off, and on seeing him swooned away. When they brought her to again she begged to be allowed to speak with him once more, and give him counsel. Being, therefore, brought under the gallows, she clasped her hands together, and, raising them up, made him a long speech with tears, recounting all their love which they had had towards each other from their youth upwards, and begged him only to say one word, that he would become a Mahometan. Amongst other things, she said to him as follows:—"But thou hast always had a compassionate heart towards me; how, then, has it turned to stone against me, seeing death before thine eyes? Alas! what, then, thinkest thou? Why art thou not in thy right mind, that thou wilt not speak to me? Alas! cursed be that love which I had for thee!"

And, being enraged at him, because he would neither speak to her nor turn Mahometan, she immediately changed her love into hatred, and said to him:—"Never wert thou worthy that I should love thee so with my whole heart. Dog! traitor! pagan! Jew! die, since thou desirest thus to die; only, O that I could be freed from this terrible death, which I shall suffer guiltless on thy account! Alas! comfort me some of you, dear people!" Having said this she swooned away.

The Turks, seeing that the young man would not be converted, angrily gnashed their teeth at him, and cried out that he should be thrown on a hook. Two executioners then standing on the gallows raised him about half an ell above a hook, and threw him on to it. This having been done, all the women and men also surrounded the lady, and, had there not been so strong a guard, they would not have allowed her to be drowned, and, had the chiaous met them, he would have been torn to pieces, like the celebrated Orpheus, by the infuriated women, or stoned by the Turks, who vehemently reviled him. When the lady had ended her prayers, the women took leave of her with great shrieking and weeping, although she was already quite unconscious, and as pale as a white sheet. An executioner took her down from the mule, tied her hands with one cloth, passed another round her waist, and fastened a third round her feet. He then placed her with her mouth downwards in a small boat, and rowing about two fathoms from the shore, for the gallows was close to the sea-shore, fixed a long staff in the cloth round her waist, pushed her lightly out of the boat into the sea, and held her under water till she was drowned. Then bringing a bier, and wrapping the corpse in a winding-sheet, they accompanied her to the tomb with Turkish honours. The poor young man lived hanging on the hook till the third day, and complained of great thirst, begging them to give him water, but nobody ventured to do so. On the third night some one, moved with compassion towards him, shot him through the head; but it was impossible to ascertain who it was that did it.

Another time they brought to execution the former Voyvode of Wallachia, who was going to excite the people to revolt against the Turkish emperor, and against the voyvode who had been put in his place, wishing to be voyvode again himself; but the Wallachians cut off his nose and ears and sent him to Constantinople, where the Emperor without mercy commanded him to be hung upon a hook. He was a well-made and handsome man, and knew several languages, particularly Latin, Greek, Italian, and Hungarian. We also several times saw Turks decapitated and hung. In the case of some of them they tied their hands and feet, and, after cutting their throats, like calves, let them lie and struggle till the blood ceased to flow. A cord was thrown over the neck of another as he stood on the ground, the other end of which was passed over a beam, and he was lifted about a span from the ground, and there allowed to hang. It is a certain truth that the Turks do not jest with malefactors, but make an end of them speedily.

When we had seen everything that we were permitted to see, both in the city and round the city, we asked our janissary, Mustapha, if it could be done without danger, to show us some handsome Turkish woman, that we might also know whether the women there are beautiful.

H

A few days after he invited us to make an excursion by
sea to a certain garden; and we got into a boat with
him, and with the other janissaries, sailed to the garden,
and entered it. The janissaries, leaving us in the garden with their servant, went into a second garden, in
which they stayed a long time, and, on returning, invited
us to go with them, saying that their female friends
were there. We Christians—there were only four of
us—went into the garden, and saw at a distance five or
six Turkish women walking about in the garden. Our
janissary's servant had a pipe, made of reeds, like an
organ, on which he piped a Turkish tune. At this the
women were apparently terrified, and looked to see
who and where the piper was; but our janissary, stepping out and showing himself, bent his head to his
knees, kissed the hand of each, and begged them not to
take it ill that he had brought four giaours, or Christians, into the garden. After conversing with the ladies
a tolerably long time, he called to us to come to him.
We came to them, and, kissing their hands, said in excuse that we had not been aware of their presence, and
begged that our conduct might not be annoying to them.
Not far off was a summer-house, which the ladies entered. We followed, and conversed with them as well as
we could, and what they did not understand in our conversation our janissary explained to them. At length,
at his urgent request, all but one unveiled; but we saw
nothing particularly beautiful in them. All were brown,
and black-eyed, and had dyed hair and eye-brows. They
caused apples, oranges, and other fruit to be brought, and
requested us to eat. After staying there a short time
we took leave of them and departed.

I cannot here forbear relating the history of a Turkish lady who was acquainted with our janissary, Mustapha. She was young and tolerably good-looking. Once upon a time Mustapha invited her to an afternoon entertainment, and I provided him for the purpose with the best wine and confectionary. He was particularly kind to me as being a Bohemian. This lady had a very aged husband, who put very little confidence in her. Not knowing how to manage to be in time for the entertainment at the appointed hour, about vespers, (for then our chiaous usually went out to prayers,) she told her husband that she was going to the bath. She took with her two captive serving-women, who carried her dresses, as usual, on their heads, in copper-pails covered with carpets, and walked behind her past our hotel, not far from which stands the handsome female bathing-house which was built by Ruska, the wife of the Turkish sultan, into which no man is allowed to go under pain of death. As she went past our hotel the lady gave notice to the janissary that she would come to the entertainment. Her distrustful husband walked a little way behind her, and, as she went into the bath, posted himself opposite, and waited for her. But who can frustrate a woman's cunning? She walked past our house in a green dress, but dressed herself in other clothes which she had brought with her, and, leaving her attendants at the bath, walked out, and came to the janissary in a red dress. He received and welcomed her in his apartment, entertained her well, and, after supper, let her out again by the little door. She went to the bath a second time, bathed, and returned home with her husband. I could not sufficiently admire this woman's cunning, and often laughed with the janissary over the recollection of it.

Meanwhile, my lord our ambassador bought six extremely beautiful Turkish horses, one of which, a grey, was particularly handsome, and cost 100 ducats. He also ordered two sets of horse-furniture to be made, which cost him full 2,000 ducats; and when he rode anywhere on that horse he had spectators and enviers enough, who said so loudly that it was a great shame for a giaour to ride on such a horse that it eventually reached my lord's ears. This horse was specially entrusted to me, to see that the grooms attended to it diligently. I rode it every week when we went out riding with the janissary, and used to race with the Turks on the open space of the hippodrome, or almeydan. On it I often raced, and won a supper from the Turks, which they caused to be prepared not far from our house, and we invited them to us in return, and entertained them well. Thus we spent this year in joy and merriment, so that we did not even wish for a better mode of life.

Immediately the year was out it began to go otherwise with us, for the tribute, which ought to have been paid annually, was not sent, because Hassan Pasha had made an incursion into Croatia, taken the castle of Wyhysht in Croatia, and brought, with great rejoicing, 300 Christian prisoners to Constantinople, each of whom was compelled to carry five or six stuffed heads of slaughtered Christians. The Turks, on their return from Croatia with their booty and captives, rode past our house, wearing on their turbans Brunswick hats, having by their sides large silver-sheathed daggers, scymitars ornamented with silver, and carrying spears and battle-

axes. Before them rode two German trumpeters blowing their trumpets, and after them went a drummer with
a drum, and a piper with a rustic pipe. After them came
some hundreds of carriages, on which were many hundred women, children, girls and boys, on whom it was
melancholy to gaze, and especially to see how mothers
took care of their children still at the breast, and held
by the hand, or carried, other little things of one or two
years old. Some old grandmothers were lamenting aloud,
and wailing as they held in their hands the heads of their
slaughtered husbands.   Then there was shouting and
exultation on the part of the Turks, who were delighted
at the victory, and lauded Hassan Pasha for having
sent these Christians to Constantinople, as a conqueror,
crying out :—" *Asserim Hassan Bassa !*"   " God help
Hassan Pasha !"   In the morning they led away the
tithe of the captives, which belonged to the Emperor,
and sent the remainder for sale to *Aurat-bazar*, or woman-market.   It is, indeed, a melancholy sight in that
market-place, when a Christian is the spectator, how his
fellow-Christian is there sold, and how he is dealt with ;
for there one buys the mother, another the child, another
a boy, another a girl, and thus they are dispersed into
different countries, and never meet each other again till
death.

In this market, in one place sit old men, in another
young men of ripe age, in another place boys ; there sit
girls, here old women, there young girls, and in another
place women suckling their children.   Whoever wishes
to purchase a captive leads him into one of the separate
rooms, which are built on the market-place, strips him
naked, inspects all his limbs, and, if he likes him, buys

him; if not, goes away and looks at others, so that these unhappy people are almost every hour obliged to strip themselves of their clothes. Their food is a piece of bread, and a draught of water, and that scantily supplied. No one who has not experienced it will believe, and it is impossible to believe, how great is the misery of Turkish captives, whom the Turks value less than dogs. As long as a captive lives, so long must he work, and when he cannot work his head is cut off; truly, more fortunate is the man who desires to die in war, rather than fall into such cruel misery, as he must endure both day and night.

At this time our fortune was already beginning to creak, when the janissaries quarrelled with the defterdar, or chief tax-gatherer, on account of non-payment of their wages, and, rising in mutiny, slew his family, to the number of seven persons. This mutiny was with difficulty appeased by the chief-pasha, and the chiaous-pasha was dismissed from all his offices for not having prevented it. My lord our ambassador, knowing very well that the Turks were preparing for war, and wishing to know what plans were being formed at the Turkish court in secret councils with regard to Hungary, induced, by many gifts and payments, the agas, or imperial chamberlains, to send him, by an old woman, information of the intentions of the Turkish court; and they then informed him, amongst other things, that it was determined, in the secret council, to commence war in Hungary.

My lord, therefore, quickly gave notice to our Emperor, by way of Venice, to be on the look out in Hungary. And not only were the imperial chamberlains induced by bribes to give information, but even the Emperor's mother herself made known to my lord the resident, through a Jewess, what she had heard from the Emperor with regard to Hungary. The Jewess was well rewarded by my lord, and brought this treasonable intelligence not to our house, but secretly to another place. The chief Turkish officials, also, informed my lord that Hassan Pasha was to march to Siseck, and take it by force. In fact, he did march to Siseck with a great number of people, and did a great deal of damage; but by the help of a merciful God, who was pleased to succour our Christians, of whom there was but a small handful, Hassan himself, his best soldiers, and a great number of chosen Turks, were slain by our men. When this news arrived at Constantinople all the city was turned to grief, and as they had before cried joyfully :—"*Asserim Hassan Bassa!*" *i. e.* "God help Hassan Pasha!" so now they lamented mournfully :—"*Hai, hai, Hassan Bassa, junacher sei!*" that is to say, "Hey, hey, Hassan Pasha, 'tis a pity that thou art slain!"

Understanding, therefore, and seeing that there would not be much jesting, I wished to go with Armenian merchants by land through Persia to Egypt, and afterwards to Jerusalem, from Jerusalem to sail to Venice by sea, and thence to travel home. I also gradually provided myself with all necessaries for the journey, and was only waiting for a safe opportunity. My lord was willing to advance me money, and I wrote home to my friends to send me some; for my greatest wish was, if it had pleased the Lord God, to perform such a journey and expedition into those unknown lands. But such was

not the will of God. At that time, too, the sister of the
Turkish emperor, whose son had fallen with Hassan
in the battle, on hearing the news, ran to the Emperor,
with dishevelled hair, as though frantic, and, falling at
his feet, demanded vengeance on the Christians.

Our ambassador, on being several times reproached
with the delay of the annual present, answered that
the Turks were in fault themselves, since they had
violated the armistice and truce, had taken the fortress
of Wyhysht in Croatia, and had taken many hundred
people captive. Wishing, however, to appease the
Turks, who were enraged at this answer, he requested
that permission might be given him to send some of his
attachés to Vienna. When this was obtained, John
Perlinger, John Malowetz, and Gabriel Hahn, the
secretary, were sent off post-haste to inform the Emperor
of what was projecting at the Turkish court. The
two former returned again, and a certain Bon-Omo*
was sent as secretary. After a quarter of a year it
could not be kept secret, but was universally said that
there would be open war in Hungary. Synan Pasha,
too, the chief enemy of the Christians, was summoned
to the Turkish emperor, and was made vizier, or generalissimo of the army in the field. He came at night
to the imperial court with a great number of lighted
torches, and was splendidly escorted to his own palace;
and everywhere, too, throughout the city resounded
shouting, wishing of good-luck, and running out of doors
with lights.

At this time Herr Karl Zahradetzky, from Moravia,
came to us by sea, being on a pilgrimage from Venice

* This is the orthography of the original.

to Jerusalem. Feeling no small deficiency in his health, he did not venture to undertake so long a sea-voyage, but stayed in our house, and bought everything necessary, intending to return to Christendom by way of Venice. In fact, before Synan Pasha was made vizier, he had obtained letters permissory, enabling him to sail to Venice without danger, and having all his things ready packed up, was intending to start the next day. Just then Synan Pasha sent straight to us, and, in order that my lord the ambassador might come to him without delay, ordered him to be told that some necessary business required his presence. My lord the ambassador immediately had a black horse brought for him, which would not in any wise allow him to mount, and he, therefore, ordered another, the grey horse, to be saddled. When we rode to the pasha, Herr Zahradetzky wished once more to accompany my lord, and wait upon him for the last time. Our ambassador, on arriving at Synan Pasha's, wished him joy of his new office, and declared that he was greatly delighted at his promotion. Synan smiled, and asked loudly:—"But art thou then very glad thereat? Thou oughtest not, indeed, to be delighted at aught, for I shall be more harmful than beneficial to thee and all giaours." He then complained vehemently, and asked why the present was not brought, saying that our ambassador, as well as his suite, must pay for it with their necks. But my lord boldly proved to him that the Turks were the cause themselves, by having violated the truce. Let them return what they had taken from our people, and observe the armistice steadfastly, and the present would be sent without delay. Synan replied again, angrily:—"Return also those youths and valiant men who have been slain by your people in Hungary, one of whom was better than all the giaours put together." He also uttered great threats, and angrily revealed his evil intent and wish to be revenged upon us, infuriating himself till he turned pale. My lord the ambassador, seeing him enraged, did not choose to dispute with him, but only said, moderately :—" Until the truce is renewed, and is steadfastly and honestly observed, and the fortresses which have been taken are restored, no tribute will be sent."

When we were about to return home there occurred a manifest token of our future misfortune. The grey horse, on which my lord rode, would in nowise allow itself to be mounted ; but bit, kicked, and reared, though it had never before done anything of the sort. My lord the ambassador was, therefore, obliged to mount his steward's horse, and ride home. When we arrived at our house the gate was immediately fastened up with iron bolts, by order of Synan, and thus the unfortunate Zahradetzky, through staying a few weeks with us in order to see the city, was compelled to remain in the house with us, and experience all our misfortunes and grievous imprisonment ; for now the Turks refused to allow him to quit the house.

We were now deprived of our allowance of provisions and everything else, and so little was given us that my lord the ambassador was obliged to send a chiaous to the pasha, and ask for permission to send out and purchase necessaries in the market with his own money. Permission was given for the clerk of the kitchen to go daily with a janissary to the market, but nowhere else, and buy necessaries. Strict orders were, moreover,

given to the janissary not to allow the clerk to speak
with any other Christians, or deliver them letters.
Thus we remained shut up in the house, as in a prison,
and no one could go out any whither.

At that time there was so great a pestilence in Constantinople that, as the Turks told us, 80,000 people
died of the plague ; and, in fact, as we ourselves saw
from our house, people were carried in large numbers,
all day long, to the grave, and even in some houses we
saw two, three, or four corpses at a time being washed,
fomented, and purified with warm water. It is certain
that it was very grievous to us when we could see nothing else but a multitude of dead bodies. Out of our
own house there died about six persons of the infection
of the plague, although we used all kinds of medicines
daily. We had the bodies buried in the city of Galata,
according to the permission granted us. The corpses
were only attended by three or four persons, and the
Franciscan monks, who have six convents there, performed the funeral ceremonies. At this time more than
half of us fell sick with the stench and with fright. I,
too, had first an ague, and then a diarrhœa, and was so
seriously ill for many weeks that the physicians despaired of my recovery, and said it was impossible for
me to get well any more.

During the time of this plague, for about four or five
months, nothing was said about the war ; but, as soon as
it passed over, proclamation was publicly made in the
streets to prepare for war against the giaours and the
Viennese king, and that considerable booty would be
obtained. After no long time a number of soldiers
marched into the city from all parts, walked and rode

about the city in large bodies, and when they saw any
of us at the windows, made signs that they would slay
us. In a word, every preparation was made for a great
war. My lord wishing to ascertain everything exactly,
who would be the leader of the host, and how strong
they would march, did not spare money, laid out large
sums on spies, obtained a clandestine knowledge of many
select plans, and of the intentions of the Turkish court,
wrote it all out with his own hand, and afterwards ordered his secretary to translate it into ciphers, wishing
to bring it as soon as possible to the knowledge of our
Emperor. These secret writings were kept in a room
under the ground, in a safe place, with such secresy that
nobody knew what and of what nature they were; and
although the steward sometimes saw the persons who
brought the intelligence, yet he could not ascertain
anything.

BOOK III.

*Of the Arrest and Imprisonment of our whole
Embassy.*

EANWHILE it happened that our
steward, Ladislaw Mörthen, committed
a capital crime, and was confined to his
apartment on parole by my lord the ambassador. The Turks had fastened up
the door of our house with bolts on the outside, and we
also secured it inside, that they might not be able to
come to us, if they wished. My lord gave the key of
the gate to the clerk of the kitchen, and ordered him to
let no one out of, or into, the house without his permission.

Meanwhile the steward, no watch being kept over him,
took advantage of the clerk's going out early in the
morning to purchase necessaries, sneaked behind, unexpectedly pushed before him, sprang out into the street,
and shouted at the top of his voice that he wished to
become a Mussulman. The chiaous who was on guard
by our house heard this exclamation with great joy,
and immediately conducted the steward to a pasha, and
laid before him the intentions of the godless villain.

The pasha not only greatly commended it, but was delighted at obtaining so important a proselyte as the steward of the Christian embassy, and immediately gave him a handsome red Turkish dress, a turban, and a fine Turkish horse, and ordered him to be conducted to circumcision with great pomp.

When this wretch was led to circumcision many hundred horse and foot soldiers went before and behind him past our house, all shouting ferociously, and wishing him joy, while he exhibited a joyful countenance, looked in at the windows, and carried himself haughtily. After circumcision, pay, or wages, amounting to forty aspers a day, as they told us, was assigned to him, which is, certainly, high pay among them. This renegade, although he had at Prague a wife, a young court lady, Madame Von Bernstein, who was in office at court as mistress-of-the-robes, and a son, a handsome youth, yet forsook all, forgot his soul and wife, took immediately a Turkish woman to wife, and frequently walked and rode past our house.

One day this steward went to Synan Pasha and said:— " As, when a Christian, I kept faith with my king, now, too, that I am a Mussulman, I wish to exhibit the same fidelity towards the Sultan and all the pashas, and will not spare anything, not even my neck, for the extension of their dominions. In order, therefore, that I may prove this fidelity to my Emperor, and the whole Turkish nation, I request that the mighty pasha do permit me, with some Turks, to examine the chancery of the ambassador of the Christian emperor, wherein I desire to find and lay before the pasha such things that every one will wonder in what way and how the

Christian ambassador came by them; for even persons of
high rank, and imperial officials, are not ashamed of
acting contrary to their conscience, and revealing to him
secret counsels, whereof, if the Viennese king knows,
there is no doubt that he will, in good time, make preparations corresponding to those of the Turks, and will
demand all possible aid from the empire."

The pasha, having thought this over, commended him
for such fidelity, and not only granted him power to
examine the chancery of the Christian ambassador, but
also assigned him some of the chief chiaouses, among
whom were a Spaniard, and several Italian renegades,
with orders that everything was to be carefully examined, and took care that no obstacle should be placed
in the way of that rascal of a steward, to whom, at his
perversion, the Turks had given the name of Ali Beg.

The day before this my lord the ambassador ordered
the documents, which had been translated into cipher,
to be brought him by the secretary, who was playing
for ducats with the rest of my lord's attendants of
equestrian rank.   On looking into them it appeared to
him that something had been left out, and he therefore
ordered the originals to be brought him out of the secret
receptacles; but, finding that there was no error in any
respect, he directed them to be immediately concealed in
the same secret places.   But the secretary liked play
better, and, forgetting his duty and the oath which he
had sworn to the Lord God and his Imperial Majesty,
thrust them into the nearest cupboard as soon as he entered the chancery, and went out again to his game.
Thus, as is manifest, no human counsel and vigilance
can hinder the judgment and ordinance of God.

The next day, very early in the morning, came this unhappy Ali Beg, with fifteen Turks of rank, to our house and knocked at the door. The clerk of the kitchen had previously had the key, but had then left it lying on a block in the kitchen. The cook, without asking anybody whether he was to open it or no, took the key in answer to the knocking, and opened the door to them. They then entered the house very quietly, and pushed unexpectedly into my lord's room, at which my lord and we were all terrified. The principal chiaous immediately informed my lord, in Italian, that they had been sent with Ali Beg by the great Synan Pasha with orders that, whereas information had reached Synan that he was about to disclose all manner of plans of theirs, and to make known to his king what was passing at the court of their most mighty Emperor, he was, therefore, to allow his chancery to be opened, and not to hinder the said Ali Beg from examining everything, and that these, indeed, were the strict orders of the pasha.

My lord the ambassador, after hearing this speech out, ordered sweet beverages and sweetmeats to be brought, and requested them to sit down. He then replied to the order of the pasha to the following effect, saying how improper a thing it was that the chancery of the ambassador of the Roman emperor should be searched, and that on the bare calumny of such an untrustworthy rascal as his former steward. So, too, he immediately reproached him and set before his eyes how he had had the heart to forget his soul, his wife, and his children, and that he would surely not escape the vengeance of God. But the Turks who were present advised my lord not to reproach him, but to leave him alone, as he was no more his servant, but a Mussulman, and required that the chancery should be opened, and themselves allowed to fulfil the will of the pasha. My lord, not being able to do otherwise, sent to the secretary, and asked him secretly whether those things (meaning the original documents) of which he well knew were in security? He, as he sat at cards, bid my lord, in answer, not to be anxious, and also coming himself to my lord, gave him a token that all was secure; and, indeed, it pleased the Lord God for our sins to deprive him of all recollection.

When, therefore, the chiaouses required the chancery to be opened, my lord ordered his secretary so to do, entered with them himself, and continually reproached the knave, teasing him, and saying that he would find important secrets, and would thereby obtain great favour with the pasha, or with the Sultan, asking him, also, to impart some of them to him. He also scornfully advised him to be sure and search well, saying that he trusted the Lord God, and felt sure he would find nothing suspicious, and told him that he (my lord the ambassador) wished to bring him to such a point, that for such lying information, and for the insult which was inflicted upon an ambassador, he should be punished, and hoisted on a hook.

In answer to this the wretched renegade said nothing but, "Only let me look!" And my lord replied to him:—"Thou findest that thou drankest thy last cup in Silesia."* When the chancery was opened, he

* I can find no explanation of this, which is evidently a proverbial expression. The German translator seems to have found it as difficult as myself, and has simply omitted it.

I

searched on, with great terror, till he trembled from head to foot, and found only some simple letters, which our comrades and acquaintances had written to us from Vienna. When the strong boxes were opened for him, he found in them a simple account of receipts and payments, and something else, which was not worth anything. And my lord ceased not to torment him, always telling him, scornfully, to look better, till he discovered the secrets, and brought the pasha the important things in return for which he would be presented with the gallows.

Then, when already about to leave the chancery, the villain espied a cupboard by the door, and ordered it to be opened for him. Then, first, the secretary recollected himself, and remembered that he had left all the most important things lying in it, and looked at my lord. My lord, imagining that those things were concealed in the proper place, and as it did not even occur to him that his secretary could have been so careless, insulted the traitor with a laugh, and the jeering exclamation, " Here they'll be ! here they'll be found !" and, smiling, ordered the cupboard to be opened. But, as soon as Ali Beg put his hand into it, he lighted upon the original documents, about six sheets thick, and drew them out of the cupboard. My lord recognized them, and turned as white as a sheet, and being unable to support himself, leant against the wall. The unhappy steward looked at them, and cried out, " I will have this and nothing more !" and, going out of the chancery in quite a cheerful mood, boasted of his success before the Turks. Although many of us were present, we did not know what the wretch had taken, nor of what he was boasting, or, certainly, had we known it, we should have wrested it from him by force, and thrown it into the fire, for we were as numerous as they. But my lord immediately began negotiating with the chiaouses, and sent his cousin to the money-chest, and ordered him to bring out dollars and ducats in Hungarian hats, and distributed them among the chiaouses, begging them only to allow him to tear something out. This would certainly have been done for the money, but that villain, when the chief chiaous requested it from him, would let nothing go out of his hands, affirming that his fortune and life depended on it. Thus my lord distributed his money to the chiaouses in vain.

When the Turkish commissaries took their departure, my lord began to lament bitterly, reproached the secretary with tears, and asked him how he should answer for it to God and our Emperor, saying,—" I care not for my own neck; I am quite content to die, if only it were not for you young people; for you will be obliged to become Mahometans to save your lives, and thus you will come to perish everlastingly owing to my heedless secretary's gaming. For, when what that unhappy renegade took out of the cupboard is brought to Synan Pasha, it is impossible for you to escape a terrible death." From that time forth he ate and drank nothing, did not sleep in bed, was continually praying with tears, and expecting every hour the time when we should be sent for.

After a short time that wretched renegade steward sent word to my lord that he would allow him to tear something out of the documents, if he would send him 1,000 broad dollars. My lord, in fact, sent him several hundred dollars; but he took the money, went with it to Synan Pasha, and boasted to him how well and honestly he meant by him, showing the money which my lord the ambassador had sent him, in order that he might permit him to erase or tear something out, saying that he would not do this for any presents, but that he had delivered to him (Synan Pasha) what he had found by search in the chancery, and humbly begging him to speak to the Emperor on his behalf, and obtain some favour for him.

The pasha without delay sent for German renegades, and had the documents translated into the Turkish language. Observing, however, that many of the chief officials, and the Sultana herself, were implicated, like an old fox, not wishing to fall into disfavour with the imperial ladies, for the Emperor's mother and wife ruled everything, and did what they liked, he kept this to himself, made little noise about it, and only informed the Sultan that secret writings had been found in the chancery of the Viennese ambassador, whence thus much could be ascertained, viz. that the ambassador betrayed to the Viennese king everything that took place in the city. He, therefore, inquired of the Emperor what should be done further in the matter. The Sultan immediately placed my lord the ambassador, and all his people and servants, in the pasha's hands, to do with them what he pleased. From this time forth they gave us no more food, save only bread and water, did not allow the clerk of the kitchen to go out to market for necessaries, and secured our house well with a guard, to prevent any one from going out of it. My lord the ambassador, expecting every hour great danger for himself and all of us, fell extremely ill with a quinsy, and did not leave his bed for some time. More

than half of us were also ill, and there remained very
few who enjoyed perfect health.   Here our best medicine was good Greek wine, of which we had as many as
sixty casks, with which many of us shortened the
mournful time, and made themselves merry, while others,
who were sick, wished for the happy hour [of death] to
come.   Thus, too, my lord the ambassador, and we who
were sick, received the last holy unction from our
priest, and commended ourselves to the Lord God.

When all things necessary for the campaign in Hungary were ready, Synan Pasha, on the 15th of August,
after kissing the Sultan's hand, and receiving the generalissimo's flag and sabre, rode very magnificently out
of the city past our house, accompanied by all the
pashas and almost all the city.   Before him rode his
dervishlars and hodzalars, and also Mahomet's friends
in green vests.   Next walked naked monks, holding
each other by the hand, and turning round, crying out,
Allah hu, till, through great exhaustion, they fell on the
ground and were obliged to lie there; others wished
him good fortune, at the top of their voices, and their
priests, the poplaslars, went before him singing and
bearing open books.   Behind him rode about twenty-
four *iltzoglans*, or sultan's pages, on very handsome
horses, all dressed in gold brocade; their stirrups,
saddles, shields, and everything on their horses glittered
with gold and precious stones, especially the lances and
sabres set with jewels.   It was, moreover, an extraor-
dinarily beautiful, warm, and pleasant day, so that when
the sun shone on those lads a great glitter was reflected
from the gold and precious stones.   Indeed, it was a
wonderful sight, when, over and above that great pomp, a

countless number of the inhabitants accompanied Synan to the place behind the city, where he had ordered his tents to be pitched and had his camp. For, whenever the Turks go from home, they do not go far on the first day, in order that, should they have forgotten anything, and it not be at hand, they may be the nearer, and therefore the more easily able to set matters to rights and fetch it.

We were all glad that our principal enemy had left the city, imagining that we should stay in the house shut up as it was, and that nothing worse would befall us; but hope deceived us. For on the third day Synan Pasha cunningly and falsely sent, in Ferhat Pasha's name, some Turks of rank to my lord the ambassador, who lay very sick, bidding him immediately to take two or three servants only and come to him (Ferhat Pasha), to translate to him some Latin documents which had been found. My lord, being more dead than alive, begged them to make his excuses to the pasha, saying that it was impossible for him to ride on horseback at that time; but as soon as he was better he would gladly visit him. But they persisted in requiring him to get ready, and said that, if he did not do so voluntarily, they would compel him, as they had a carriage for him with them. My lord the ambassador, seeing that it could not be otherwise, put on a black velvet Hungarian suit, and, as the Turks told him he would come back in about an hour, seated himself in the carriage, which was lined with red cloth, (like those which have been used in cities from time immemorial, and into which you get by steps,) and bidding adieu to us, was taken from us by a pair of horses, not to Ferhat, but out of the city to Synan Pasha, only having five

persons of his suite with him. On arriving at the camp
the Turks immediately placed him, as being an invalid,
in a tent, and his attendants in irons, securing them
all with a guard of janissaries. We, however, who remained at the house had no knowledge whither my
lord had gone.

After about two hours we saw people running from
all quarters by thousands to our house, placing themselves in rows, and creeping on the roofs, and at last so
many collected that we could not see to the end of them.
Not knowing what this indicated, and what kind of
spectacle was about to be exhibited, we imagined at
first that some part of our house was on fire; till, after
a short time, we saw the guard which was usually employed at executions making straight for our hotel.
Behind this guard rode the sub-pasha, the judges, the
head-executioners, heralds, and under-executioners, bearing fetters in their hands. The eyes of all the people
were then directed upon us. When they arrived at the
house, the sub-pasha and the other Turks dismounted;
the janissaries opened our house with a noise and shout
(a thing which we did not expect, but imagined that my
lord would come to us again), and led and dragged all
of us, wherever they could seize us, down the galleries and
out of the house. They then threw an iron ring over the
neck of each and passed a chain through it. Upon this
each of us fled hither and thither wherever we could,
as though we were mad. Though I had been some
weeks ill of dysentery, and could not stand on my feet,
nevertheless, seeing what was happening to my comrades,
I did not remain in bed, but crept up as high as possible
under the rafters, springing from one to the other in

such a dangerous manner, that, if I had fallen, I should
have been dashed into a hundred pieces. Finally, I
crept quite unconsciously back to my bed; and when
the Turks had already got all my companions fastened
by chains, and had also laid their hands on and divided
everything they could find, the sub-pasha came to me, and
one said to him :—" This lad is young and sick, he must
get well and become a Mussulman; let us leave him
here till we return, and place him in Ferhat Pasha's
serail."

On hearing this, for I had already learnt some Turkish, I got out of bed, and told them that I was willing
to suffer evil and good with my comrades, and would not
stay, begging them, for God's sake, not to leave me there.
Thus in my shirt, and without my trousers, taking only a
long Hungarian mantle, I was led down to the place
where my comrades were already fettered by the neck.
On coming down I fell to the ground, and was unable to
rise. Meanwhile, one of the executioners ran up and
put an iron ring round my neck, intending also to pass
a chain through it, but the chiaous bade him leave it as
it was, saying that I could not walk for illness.

They then opened the door, and counted us out, one
after the other, for they had a list of us all.   Then an
executioner took each by his iron ring, the sub-pasha
mounted his horse, the guards began to close round us,
and make a way through the people. As I could not
stand upon my feet, they brought me a Turk, whom
they call a *hamola*, or porter, who carries all manner of
things from the sea about the city for hire, on whose
pannier, which was stuffed with rushes, they perched me
like a landrail, and I sat upon it like a dog on a bank.

Meanwhile, a dwarfish Turk, with a reddish beard, called out at the top of his voice to the bystanders:—" Is it right that this true believer should carry that dog ?" And, running up to me, he gave me a violent blow, so that I shot down from my steed I knew not how ; also he contemptuously kicked me in the side, and would have beaten me still more, had not our former janissary, Mustapha, seen it, and taken compassion upon me. Not enduring this conduct, and looking upon me with sorrow,—for he wished me everything that was good,— he flourished his staff, and dragging me from him, re- viled him in Turkish, asking him why he struck a poor sick prisoner, and wanted to show his manhood on me? If he possessed so heroic a heart, let him take it against fresh and strong giaours in Hungary ; he would find plenty of them to match themselves with him ; it was easy (pointing at me) to beat and maltreat a dying giaour.   And when the other answered him contuma- ciously, my friend the janissary cudgelled him with his staff over the head, till the blood streamed, upon which the Turk rushed at the janissary with a knife. In a moment about a hundred people ranged themselves on the side of the janissary, and as many more on the side of the other, and they were already beginning to take up stones and throw them at each other.   Indeed, had not the guards, and the imperial judge, or sub-pasha, speedily turned and galloped to us, and ordered them to keep the peace under pain of death, a great riot would have taken place on my account, and we should all have had to suffer for it guiltless.

When this disturbance was quieted, Mustapha raised me from the ground, and gave me to two men to lead ;

but, as I could not walk for exhaustion, I tottered on a long way behind the rest.   Meanwhile, we met a number of muleteers, taking wood, fastened on their mules with ropes, to the court.   A chiaous cut the ropes, and ordered me to be placed on a mule.   One executioner held me by one foot, another by the other, that I might not fall off.   My comrades they led in a row by three chains, and I rode honourably after them, only in my shirt, and that very comfortably, on my prickly wooden saddle.   They led us, for greater disgrace and ridicule, through the most populous squares and streets, and it was very hot weather, so that we could have died for excessive thirst.   Some pitied us, others gnashed their teeth at us, and said the best place we could go to was the gallows.   When they had led us up and down the city to their satisfaction, they conducted us straight to the sand-gate, where the fish-market is held.   On both sides of us, in front and behind, walked a countless multitude of people, for never before had so many persons been seen led to execution at once.

The press of people crowding out through the gate hindered our conductors, so that they were obliged to stop with us in front of the gate.   For my own part, sick and tormented by great exhaustion, thirst, and heat, as I was, and, moreover, with my skin torn off by the saddle till I bled, I could not recollect where we were.   Looking round I saw John von Winorz, the priest, and asked him where we were.   He answered that we were not far from the gallows, and, therefore, had better resign ourselves to the will of God, and commit our souls to Him.   Meanwhile, we kept advancing further, the janissaries making a road for us by the use of their sticks. When I saw the hooks on the gallows, and two executioners upon it holding the pullies, I immediately lost my self-command, swooned, and became entirely unconscious. Nor did we expect aught else than that they would hang us all up, since that was exactly the course of proceeding which they observed with others at their execution.

My comrades related to me afterwards (for, as aforesaid, I had lost the power of thought and recollection, as well as sensation) that, when they brought us under the gallows, two more executioners climbed up, and meanwhile a judge addressed us to the following effect, telling us that we saw a terrible death before our eyes, and, therefore, for the great compassion which he felt for us, promised, by the head of the Sultan, his lord, that our lives should be granted us if we would but turn Mahometans. But, by the grace of God, none of us did this, but we were all ready to lose our lives in preference; although, on the other hand, we were so overwhelmed by fear of death that none of us knew whether he was alive or dead.

After remaining still about a quarter of an hour, the sub-pasha gave orders to conduct us to the sea, which was close at hand. The vulgar, therefore, as they had not hung us on the hooks, had no other expectation but that they would drown us in the sea. Every living soul, therefore, ran down to the sea, and took their seats in boats and barges, for greater convenience in looking on. When they brought us to the shore, they thrust us almost head-over-heels into a boat, in which camels and mules, with all manner of mercantile burdens, are ferried over from Europe to Asia, cursing at us, meanwhile, vehemently, and pushing us in such a manner that the poor wretches pulled each other down by their chains. Coming to myself again, I thanked my God that it had pleased Him to release me from that terrible death, and being afraid lest they should drag me from the mule, and throw me, like my comrades, into the boat, I fortunately saw a Turk whom I knew, and called out to him, imploring him:—" My soul, for God's sake I implore thee, help me !" He, although the rest looked angrily at him, and reviled him, gave no heed to them, but ran up rapidly, helped me down, and after saying to me sorrowfully, " God release thee," departed.

Having thrust off from the shore, the chief judge and his attendants sailed with us in the boat, and we had no other idea but that they would drown us, or take us to that frightful black tower, on the Black Sea, for they turned with us in that direction. Then they stopped and asked us again whether we were willing to become Turks, saying that it was now our last hour, as they were about to drown us all by Synan Pasha's orders ; that we should, therefore, have compassion on our youth, and that they were willing to make imperial gentlemen-in-waiting, spahis, and janissaries of us, and give us fine clothes and horses. But we constantly prayed to God, and, committing ourselves to Him, persevered in saying that whatever pleased His gracious Goodness should be our fate, acknowledging that we had deserved all this misery by our sins. We had spectators round us in thousands, who wished to gaze upon our watery funerals, for the upper and under executioners were also with the judge in our boat.

As soon as they saw our steadfastness, and that not

one of us would become a Turk, they threatened us,
and angrily impressed upon us that they would put us
into such a prison that, when there, we should wish to
be dead rather than alive. After bullying us till they
were satisfied, they brought us round at last to the imperial arsenal, or magazine, where there are many hundreds of various boats, and where stores of galleys, and
other military requisites are kept in vaults. Having
removed us from the boat, they conducted us into a
large square building, which was surrounded by large
walls several fathoms high. Here, at the first gate, sat
the pasha's Kihaja and the Quardian Pasha, or the
chief commander of the guards. In this enclosure there
is a third building for prisoners, into which the light
comes only from above, and which has no windows at
the sides. In the principal building there are captives of
various nations, artizans who construct galleys, and
divers other things; for instance, carpenters, joiners,
smiths, ropemakers, sailclothmakers, locksmiths, and
coopers, who are conducted every day into this or that
workshop. These are the best off of all, for they have
it in their power to filch things, sell them secretly, and
buy something to eat; nay, when they work industri-
ously, porridge is given them on Friday, (the Turkish
Sunday,) and, above all, they have hopes of release before the rest. For, when they execute a handsome
piece of work, whether it be a galley, a galleon, or any
other boat, in a masterly and artistical style, and the
pasha who commands by sea is pleased with it, he con-
fers the following favours on the chief artizans. Taking
from them a promise not to escape from Turkey for ten
years, more or less, but to work faithfully till the expi-

ration of that time, he releases them on parole, and, after that time, they can marry and settle there at their liking, or return to their own country. When, moreover, any one wishes to ransom himself, or earn his liberty, since no Turk promises for a Christian, he must produce as security ten or twenty other Christian captives, that is to say, should he during that time escape before he has earned his liberty, or should a captive who is ransoming himself not bring his price by a certain day, then these, his sureties, become liable, one to have an eye struck out, a second to have an ear, a third to have his nose, a fourth to have the thumbs of both his hands, and the toes of both his feet cut off, or the teeth on one side of his jaw knocked out, or to receive so many hundred blows on his belly, the calves of his legs, and the soles of his feet. Not till any given captive obtains such sureties (and it is seldom that any one makes such an engagement) is he released to go to Christendom, and if he is not to be found, and does not pay his ransom, his sureties have to suffer according to their bond.

In my time I saw a captive Hungarian in that prison who had become surety for a friend, who, on arriving in Christendom, like a knave as he was, forgot his benefactor and did not return. The poor surety had, therefore, for about two years, to bear two sets of fetters, his own and those of the person for whom he had made the engagement, to lose one ear, his four front teeth, both the thumbs on his hands, all the toes on his feet, and to be frightfully beaten with a stick every Friday. This continued until the late Palfi, of blessed memory, heard of it, and ordered the Hungarian, who had come from

Turkey, to be beheaded, and his ransom transmitted to Turkey. But, sad to say, that most unfortunate man had already lost his health, and deplored, above all, with tears, the loss of his thumbs and toes, and complained that he should never be able to use a weapon to the day of his death. In other respects he was a tall and well-made person, and, if that knave had not deceived him, he intended to have ransomed himself, and taken vengeance on the Turks.

Such prisoners as are priests, scribes, scholars, citizens, or gentlemen, are in the greatest misery, because they have not learnt any handicraft, and no value is set upon them. The second prison is for common prisoners who know no handicraft. Of these there were then about 700 persons, of all the various nations that there are beneath the sky. These are taken, in the beginning of spring, on board the galleys as rowers. When they return from the voyage they must hew stone and marble, construct earthworks, carry materials for building, and, in a word, like day-labourers, if there is any contemptible work to be done anywhere, they must perform it. They receive from one year's end to another nothing more for food than two loaves of bread *per diem*, and water to drink. The Turks strike and beat them like cattle for the least misconduct. Nay, not even at night do they enjoy repose, but must go to work if anybody wants them.

The third building is a hospital, in which the sick prisoners lie, and where the old men who are past work through age loiter about. These, besides bread, receive soup and porridge. This building is called Paul's prison. As long as they are there they are made comfortable; when they get well, they must work to make up

what has been neglected; if they die, they are given to
the prisoners to be buried, or thrown into the sea.
Having brought us to this place, the judges presented
letters or orders from Ferhat Pasha to the Quardian
Pasha, instructing him how we were to be dealt with.
After this the executioners took the chains and rings off
our necks, and two or three of them ran up, and tripped
up the feet of each, so that he fell on the ground. Here
we poor wretches expected that they would beat us
with a stick, but, thank God, that did not take place; but
gipsy smiths came, and putting an iron ring round the
feet of one who lay on the ground, passed a chain through
it, clinched it on an anvil, and then fastened a second,
whom he selected, by the foot to the same chain. Seeing that this was all they did, each of us had himself
coupled to the companion whom he liked best. As soon
as two were coupled together, they were obliged to go
immediately into the common prison. When all had
been thus fettered except myself and the apothecary, a
little man, who was then also ill, they fastened us together as we lay on the ground from exhaustion, though
I besought them earnestly enough, saying that we were
both ill, and could not walk, and though it was impossible for me to lift the chain. When they bade us go
into the prison, I rose with difficulty from the ground,
and immediately fell down again on my back, and was
unable to rise. A Turk, wishing to compel us to get
up, struck me with a stick over the back, bidding me
get up, and so he did the apothecary several times; but
the pasha, seeing our real weakness, ordered one Turk
to carry the chain behind us, and two others to lead us
to the prison, where I seated myself with my sick com-

panion close to the gate, for I was unable to go further, and there had my den as long as we were in that prison.

There were then but few prisoners in the gaol, for they had gone as rowers on board the war-boats, but they were from time to time expected. These prisoners had left abundant filth behind them, as well as many pieces of rags and tattered garments, which we took and placed under our heads instead of pillows. In truth, no man who has not experienced it will believe what sort of lodging it was in that prison. For, not to speak of fleas, lice, and bugs, there was a kind of black insects, like large ants, and wherever they stung blood immediately spouted out, and the place swelled up, just as when the measles break out on children. We were all so stung that nowhere over our whole persons had we a sound spot where you could stick a pin, on the head and face just as little as on the rest of the body. To us voluptuous people, unaccustomed to such lodgings, it was excessively difficult to get used to this; for, though we stripped ourselves naked, it was no good, but those flies stung us still. After all, however, it was lucky for us that it was so, for the skin over the whole of our bodies was so bestung that we no longer felt the biting of lice or bugs, although it was impossible to get used to the stinging of those other insects. The steam, stench, and heat were so excessive that I might have lost my senses, and, above all, the dysentery attacked me so violently in that prison that I could not remain a quarter of an hour in the place where I was. And thus, tortured and utterly miserable being that I was, I wished for death, especially as my companion could not walk and carry the chain, and we were obliged to defile

K

the place where we sat down, and to repose in the stench.
That day they gave us two loaves of bread each, and a
small can of water; but I dared not and could not eat or
drink anything either that day or the next, but besought
God that it might please Him to release me from my
misery by death.

The next day the chief superintendent of the prisoners
came into our prison himself with several guards, and,
seeing me lying thus naked in this wretched condition,
had compassion upon me. On seeing him standing by
me, I quickly drew my Hungarian mantle over me, and
covered myself above, having no other clothing, for none
of my comrades had taken so little clothing from home
as I. Thus covered with this mantle, I kissed the foot
of the pasha of the guard, and besought him with tears
to have compassion upon me, and, if it were possible, to
release me from the chain, so long as I was ill. But he
said,—"*Olmas, olmas, giaur!*" " It cannot, it cannot be,
pagan!" but if I wished to be fettered to some one who
was healthier and stronger, he said he would permit it.
Not knowing to whom else to have myself fettered, I
looked at our chaplain, my countryman, and asked
him to have me fettered to the *papas*, which is the
name there given to the priests. The papas, who had
a healthy companion, was anything but pleased, and
looked sour at me, but was obliged, nevertheless, to allow
himself to be fastened to me by the chain, and also to
go with me and carry the chain, whenever my illness
compelled me. At the beginning he was patient; once,
twice, a third time, he held his peace : but when he was
obliged to go with me very frequently, and with great
annoyance to himself, he began to revile me, and to call

me knave, and all kinds of foul and monstrous names, and said that he would not go with me. I, in return, exhorted him to patience, and reminded him that, as a clergyman, he ought to be an example to the rest, and said that I was not in fault for my illness; but since the Lord God had laid it upon me, sorrowful afflicted being that I was, I did not know what to do or say, and had rather either get well quickly or die. As, however, I did not cease urging him to go with me, he frequently kicked me so that I fell head-over-heels, and would not go with me after all. Once, when he was obliged to go with me and carry the chain, he threw it into all kinds of filth, wept, lamented, and complained that he should lose his health through me; but he was obliged afterwards to carry it back, filthy as it was, to our cattle-like lair, and I cleaned it again with water.*

My illness lasted several weeks, and, if it had lasted longer, I certainly should have deprived the poor chaplain of his life, for he was now so emaciated and wretched that he was bent double; for they gave us nothing but bread for food, and not enough of that to satisfy us, and with me he had no peace or repose either day or night. When at length, with a broken heart, and with tears, I implored God that it might please Him to have compassion on my great and intolerable misery, and either to restore me to health, or remove me from this world, whichever was His holy will, and my comrades, also, seeing me half dead, prayed earnestly for me to God, the good God listened to me, so that my illness ceased,

* The German translator here introduces a violent attack upon the celibacy of the clergy, and puts half a page of most pathetic rhetoric into the mouth of the author.

and I began to eat something. I crumbled a small loaf of bread into water, made porridge of it by boiling, and eat it.

As time went on I began to be much better in health, and when I imagined that it was all over, my dear companion, Mr. Chaplain, fell sick of a similar disease, while I, feeling no lice or insects any more, was sleeping and resting as pleasantly on the bare ground, after my illness, as on the best made bed, so that I had no need to use any provocatives to sleep. In this pleasant slumber the chaplain woke me, and urged me to go with him and help to carry the chain. And I went once, ten times, twenty times; but at last I got so sick of going with him that I meted out an equal measure to him, and called him a confounded silly parson, alleging that I had not tormented him before with going so much as he tormented me now; till at last we should both have been unable to bear it any longer, but must have paid for it with our lives.

The previous prisoners at length returned from rowing on board the vessels of war, and came into the gaol amongst us. Learning that we had a priest amongst us, they treated him very reverentially. Seeing him tormented by illness, all the artizans gave in a written petition to the pasha in command of the guard, and besought that the priest might be released from chains, till he recovered, engaging, on his behalf, that he should not escape. The pasha listened to their request, and ordered him to be released, and had me fettered by both feet to the chain, which I carried twice as willingly by myself as with a partner. When, by the grace of God, I got well again, without any kind of medicine, and my

stomach recovered its tone, two small loaves of bread
per diem did not suffice me.   So I learned from the
other prisoners to knit stockings, gloves, and Turkish
hats, and it pleased the Lord God to bless me so in this
handicraft that I often earned money, with which I
bought meal, porridge, oil, vinegar, olives, salad, and
bread.   Meanwhile, my former partner, Mr. Chaplain,
also recovered, and obtained me for a companion again,
and we were fettered together as before.   As he could
not weave or knit, he lived with me upon what I earned,
until all the prisoners went again before the superintendent of the guard, and humbly besought him to
allow them on certain days, which were hallowed among
Christians, to perform Divine Service before daylight,
and before they went to their work.   They offered
to give him a present for this permission, which was,
accordingly, granted them.

Many years ago there had been an altar in the common prison, consecrated by a regular bishop, and fenced
round with rails ; and the prisoners possessed, also, a
silver cup and the other requisites for the celebration of
holy mass.   On every great and apostolical festival our
chaplain, who was temporarily released from his chains,
celebrated holy mass, while I, with the chain, acted as
acolyte, sang the epistle, and gave the prisoners the
crucifix to kiss.   They contributed alms according to
their poverty, so that we always had a kreutzer or so
by us for food, and were easily able to support ourselves.
After mass the Turkish gipsies fettered the chaplain to
me again by the chain.

Once, on a festival after holy mass, a master-carpenter,
a Christian prisoner, invited the chaplain and me to

partake of a fine tabby tom-cat, which he had fed up
for a long time, and named Marko.   It was a fine and
well-fatted cat, and I saw, with my own eyes, when the
carpenter cut his throat. As my partner, Mr. Chaplain,
would not go, and fettered together as we were I could
not go without him, he sent us, as a present, a fore-
shoulder of the cat, which I ate. It was nice meat, and
I enjoyed it very much, for hunger is a capital cook, so
that nothing makes one disgusted ; and if I had only
had plenty of such tom-cats, they would have done me
no harm.

At this time, Krygala Pasha sent orders that some of
the old prisoners should be sent from our prison to his
serail or the palace of his wives, where they were to
clear out and clean up a building that had fallen into
decay.   The Turks, especially the more powerful ones,
have more than one wife ; but, although no Turk is
allowed to enter their abode, much less to talk with
them, yet in the presence of miserable captives they
are not concealed, but their wives are permitted to sport
and play tricks with them, and ridicule them as much as
they please, it being supposed that they can have no love-
passages with such sunburnt and emaciated Christians.

Amongst these prisoners, a German, Matthew Saller,
was sent to clean up in the palace. When he had been
there scarcely a fortnight he made acquaintance with
the pasha's wives, and having seen all their wardrobes,
broke open a cupboard in the night, stole out of it two
goblets, and three female girdles, each valued at 10,000
ducats, and brought them secretly, without any one's
knowledge, and with immense joy, into the prison, thinking that he should therewith be able to ransom himself

from prison. When he had cut these girdles to pieces
without being seen, and had taken off the diamonds,
rubies, emeralds, turquoises, and other ornaments, he
buried all in a can in the ground where he lay. But
fortune did not grant him his wish. For one of the
prisoners who had noticed him digging, after his departure stole the things again—one thief robbing another
—and thus he afterwards sought for the second thief
with tears, and confided to us what he had lost. Having,
however, still a small silver goblet, he sold it to a Turk
on his way to work, and thereby betrayed himself; for,
some days afterwards, the goblet was recognized, and
the question asked from whom it had come. When the
merchant confessed that he had bought it from a prisoner, and also gave that prisoner's name, Krygala
Pasha's *kihaja*, or major-domo, came with a good many
Turks, and ordered poor Matthew to be called out. He,
firmly believing that he would be hung without mercy,
resolved to die heroically, and leave his fame behind
him. When about to quit the prison, he took with him
secretly a long knife, and when he came before the
kihaja, on being asked where he had put those stolen
girdles, confessed all truly, how he certainly had stolen
them himself, and buried them in the ground, but that
he had been robbed again by another. The kihaja, therefore, commanded him to be seized, on hearing which
he unexpectedly rushed on him with the knife, intending to stab him, but was prevented by the superior
numbers of the Turks. The kihaja began to call to the
Turks to seize him, while he, springing on his feet, and
seeing that he could not escape, defended himself valiantly with the knife, and wounded several of the Turks,

till, finally, he was so overwhelmed with stones that he could not help falling to the ground. The Turks then seized him, and dragged him struggling to the major-domo, who ordered the poor wretch to receive 1,000 blows with a stick, so that he swelled up all over like a frog, or a bladder. The prisoners then took him, half buried him in a dunghill, and let him lie till the third day, when he gradually came to, like a fly, so that he did not die, but was always pale as a sheet, and had a swollen belly. Incredible, but true, that a man could suffer so much.*

At this time news arrived that our friends had obtained a glorious victory over the Turks in Hungary, and cut to pieces many thousands of them. On hearing this we were again in great terror, for the Turks looked sour at us, gnashed their teeth, and threatened to have us hung on the hooks. Then came the imperial kihaja, had us all called out, and said that they would cut off our noses and ears, because our friends, brothers, and cousins had slain so many Mussulmans. We excused ourselves as well as we could, saying that it was not our fault. On his departure others came, informing us in confidence, and assuring us with great oaths, that they were really going to cut off our noses and ears. Upon this, sorrowful and afflicted as we were, and not knowing what to do for terror, we heartily bewailed our noses and ears, and bound ourselves together by an oath

* My landlord at Cracow, in 1850, Pan Zieromski, who was taken prisoner by the Russians at the passage of the Beresina under Ney, received 800 blows for refusing to take the Russian military oath in the Caucasus, and survived, though for a year he never heard the sound of his own voice.

that, if they did this, and the Lord God permitted us to
return to Christendom, we would wage war against the
Turks to the day of our death, and whomsoever we captured we would cut off their noses and ears, and would
induce others also to do the same.

The pasha of the guard then came to our prison, bringing with him two barbers, or hair-cutters, had us all
summoned out, and ordered us all to sit down on the
ground. We all wept, and entertained no other idea
but that it would be done, as we had been told, and,
therefore, no one was willing to be the first to sit down,
until the scourge compelled us so to do. Anybody can
imagine how we, at this time, felt about the region of the
heart. We were all as pale as a sheet, and the barbers,
stepping up and seeing us so frightened, laughed heartily,
and all our stomachs began to ache. When we had
seated ourselves on the ground, instead of cutting off
our noses and ears, they shaved our heads and beards
with a razor, for some of us had their hair and beard
grown to a considerable length, and, after laughing at us
to their heart's content, bade us go back to prison.
When our terror passed away, and we looked at and saw
each other all clipped round and beardless, like so many
calves' heads, we could not help laughing, because we
could scarcely recognize one another. Neither did we
bear them any malice for the state of baldness to which
they had reduced us, and they were satisfied with having
frightened us abundantly about nothing. Afterwards
more trustworthy Turks informed us that the grand
vizier had really ordered our noses and ears to be cut
off, and ourselves to be sent, thus shamefully handled, to
Christendom; but the mufti, their chief bishop, on learn-

ing it, had opposed it, and would not allow that mal-
treatment to be inflicted upon us, as we had not waged
war against them, but had only been attached to an
embassy, and were in no wise in fault ; at any rate, he
said, it would have been a sin to maltreat us thus. The
grand vizier, not being able to revenge himself upon us in
any other way, had our heads and beards shaved with a
razor, and the next day all of us chained to the oars
amongst the other prisoners on board the galleys.

We were conducted on board the galley, or large war-
boat, under the care of a vigilant guard, and Achmet, the
reis, or captain, who commanded on board the vessel, a
Christian born in Italy, but who had now become a Turk,
immediately received us and ordered us all to be chained
to oars.   The vessel was tolerably large, and in it five
prisoners sat on a bench, pulling together at a single oar.
It is incredible how great the misery of rowing in the galleys is ;   no work in the world can be harder : for they
chain each prisoner by one foot under his seat, leaving
him so far free to move that he can get on the bench
and pull the oar.   When they are rowing, it is impossible, on account of the great heat, to pull otherwise than
naked, without any upper clothing, and with nothing on
the whole body but a pair of linen trousers.   When
such a boat sails through the Dardanelles, out of the
narrow into the broad sea, iron bracelets, or rings, are
immediately passed over the hands of each captive, that
they may not be able to resist and defend themselves
against the Turks.   And thus fettered hand and foot
the captive must row day and night, unless there is a
gale, till the skin on the body is scorched like that of a
singed hog, and cracks from the heat.   The sweat flows

into the eyes and steeps the whole body, whence arises excessive agony, especially to silken hands unaccustomed to work, on which blisters are formed from the oars, and yet give way with the oar one must; for when the superintendent of the boat sees any one taking breath, and resting, he immediately beats him, naked as he is, either with the usual galley-slave scourge, or with a wet rope dipped in the sea, till he makes abundance of bloody weals over his whole body. Under all this you must be silent, and neither look at him nor cry out " Oh !" or you have immediately twice as many blows, and these cutting words in addition:—" *Pregidy anaseny, sigligum, irlasem?*" " Ha, dog, why dost thou murmur, contradict, and get angry ?"

Thus, too, it happened to one of our company, an Austrian knight, a grey-haired man, who, when a Turk struck him with the usual scourge over the naked shoulders, cried out twice or thrice,—" Oh ! for God's sake, do not beat me !" The Turk, not understanding the language in which he spoke, imagined that he was reviling him, and therefore beat the poor wretch violently, so that he was obliged to learn patience with the rest. No man can narrate that exceeding misery, or believe that the human body, tortured with all manner of suffering, can bear and endure so much. In the first place, a man is not only baked, but even roasted, all day long by the excessive heat ; secondly, he must pull at the oar till his bones and all his veins crack ; and thirdly, every moment he must expect the usual scourge, or the dipped rope ; and frequently some jackanapes of a rascally Turkish boy amuses himself with beating the captives from bench to bench one after the other, and laughing at

them. All this you must not only bear patiently from
the snivelling rascal, and hold your tongue, but, if you
can bring yourself to it, you must kiss his hand, or foot,
and beg the dirty boy not to be angry with you. For
food nothing is given but two small cakes of biscuit.

When they sail to some island where Christians live,
you can sometimes beg, or, if you have money, buy
yourself a little wine, and sometimes a little porridge,
or soup. So too, when we rested one, two, three, or
more days by the shore, we knitted gloves and stockings of cotton, sold them, and sometimes bought ourselves additional food, which we cooked ourselves in
the vessel. Although the benches in this vessel were
somewhat small, five of us sat fettered on each. We
had also abundance of lice and bugs; but our skins and
bodies were already so covered with bites, and scorched
by the heat of the sun, that we felt little of this dis-
comfort. Each of us certainly had two blue shirts and
a reddish blouse—there were no other upper clothes—
but we only dressed ourselves in them at night. Indeed,
we had a most miserable, sorrowful life, and worse than
death, in that vessel.

Sometimes a draught of wine, which grows on the
island *Alla Marmora*, where they hew marble, and is
very good, cheered and strengthened us amidst this
torture. We likewise enjoyed the good Wallachian
cheese, which they brought from Wallachia and Moldavia
to Constantinople and sold. The Wallachians make it
in the following manner. They take a fresh skin from
a newly-killed goat, make a bag out of it with the needle,
turn the smooth side out and the hairy side in, fill it
with milk till it looks like a bagpipe-bag, sew it up, leave

the milk in it till it turns sour and mixes thoroughly with the hair, and then take it for sale. Six of us who were in partnership, having sold the gloves and stockings which we had made, bought a tolerably large piece of this cheese mixed with hair, which certainly came to us very acceptably, and tasted to us then better than macaroons; for we made soup of it, crumbled our mouldy biscuit into it, and eat it with remarkable appetite, paying no attention to and feeling no disgust at the circumstance that there were hairs in it. Ah! how many times, and indeed times out of number, did I remember, how in Bohemia they make soup of fine and good cheese even for useless greedy dogs, crumble fine bread into it, and give it them to eat; whereas, I, poor wretch, must thankfully receive such miserable hairy cheese and mouldy biscuit, and suffer hunger! Often did I wish, that, in point of food, I might be a companion to those dogs!* But for our sins it pleased the Lord God worthily and righteously to bring all this upon us; for previously, while we were living in freedom, and enjoying all manner of pleasures at Constantinople, we would not believe the statements of other captives that their life was so miserable and afflicted, until we were obliged to experience and digest it ourselves. And, in sooth, whilst a man is living in pleasure he will not believe how the poor and needy feels about the heart, and he has no compassion on him, until he experiences similar misery himself. Oh, were such a one fettered for only a fortnight to the oars!

There were also amongst our comrades several effemi-

* How this reminds one of the prodigal son, who longed " to fill his belly with the husks that the swine did eat!"

nate Austrians, who had never eaten any cheese from the
day of their birth, and who, whilst in freedom, if anybody smeared their knife or bread with cheese, made a
terrible fuss, and could not help bringing up everything
they had eaten or drunk. When these unfortunate
Austrians came on board the vessel, and saw us buying
the hairy Wallachian cheeses, at first they boldly declared that they would rather die of hunger than eat
anything so nasty; but very soon their taste altered.
For having nothing but the mouldy biscuit, and never a
sufficiency of that, and seeing us willingly and with a
good appetite eating soup made of the cheese, while they
could scarcely see out of their eyes for hunger, they
begged us to let them taste our food. After this they
would have been heartily glad to breakfast, not only on
the soup, but even on the hairy bag that contained the
cheese, if it had only been possible to procure it always.
Thus the stomach, especially when hungry, is a very
good cook; it digests everything, gets used to everything,
however disagreeable it appears at first sight, and rejects
nothing when it wants food. Indeed, necessity is a master
that teaches a man everything.

Once, too, a Turk brought a bag-full of boiled sheep's
heads for sale, and we bought the heads from him and
thanked him besides. When he was about to leave the
vessel, our superintendent met him, and asked him
who gave him leave to enter it and sell sheep's heads to
the captives without his permission? The Turk made
an angry answer to the superintendent, and received in
return a blow from his fist. Retiring back again into
the vessel he was seized by him, but struggled out
of his hands, and ran through us and escaped, to our

misfortune. The superintendent was so violently enraged at us for not seizing him that he immediately ordered six blows with the usual scourge to be given to each of us over the bare back, beginning at the first bench and ending at the last; and thus, on account of this godless villain, over three hundred poor Christian captives had to suffer. If the Turk had come to us in the boat a second time we should have felt such tender compassion for him that not a single piece of him would have remained. Being tender, I felt the effects of this beating for a tolerably long time, and so did some of the rest. Bloody weals sprang up in different parts of the body, and as it was the very hottest weather, and we were obliged to leave the island and pull at the oars, the skin burst, the perspiration aggravated the pain, it itched, it nipped, enough to drive one mad; but it pleased a kind God again to grant that I obtained favour in the eyes of a Turk, who gave me a piece of salve to put over it. Nevertheless, as I could not be free from pain, and it could not be helped, I comforted myself, at any rate, with the fact that I had three hundred partners in my pains, according to the proverb :—

> " A pleasure 'tis, when woes must be,
> A partner in your woes to see."

At this time there were sixteen important prisoners in the *Black Tower*, four Hungarians, two Greeks, one German, and the rest Italians. The Greeks were notorious pirates, or sea-robbers, who had done great damage to the Turkish merchants. And some of these prisoners had been fourteen, fifteen, and sixteen years in the tower, without having any hope of getting out of it. The two Greeks, who were famous heroes and majestic

men, had been captured by the Turks for the third time.
As they had forced their way out of prison twice, they
were placed, the third time, in the Black Tower, as
an eternal prison, and had already been there three
years; but, being very cunning, were day and night
scheming how to escape for the third time. But as no
one was allowed to go to them, and they were very well
watched by the guards, one of them fell ill, and having
some money, sent it as a present to the governor of the
Black Tower, begging him, for God's sake, to allow a
draught of wine or spirits, to be brought by a Christian.
Permission being given for this, though with great difficulty, a Greek Christian brought a small bottle of spirits
into the prison for him, and this cunning fellow immediately persuaded him to promise to deliver a small note,
which he wrote secretly, to a friend of his not far from
the island, and, in fact, he did deliver it. A few weeks
afterwards, just as the two Greek prisoners wished,
some unknown Greek peasants brought a good sheep,
some honey, rice, oil, olives, melons, and all kinds of
fruit to the governor to take what he liked of it himself,
and distribute the rest among the prisoners. These peasants also brought a small cask of wine, and requested
that it might be given to the sick as strengthening medicine, declaring that they gave it as alms on account of
their sins. The governor was delighted at these presents, took the sheep and what he liked, and sent the
prisoners the rest, though in tolerably small amount,
as well as the cask of wine, because the Turks do not
drink it. In this cask was a false bottom, under which
was concealed a letter from the friends of the two
Greeks, who asked to know what else they were to send

them into the prison.   The Greeks, without telling any of the prisoners what was going to be done further, gave written instructions to their friends.   Some weeks afterwards other Greeks came, and made a much larger present to the governor, and also sent two casks of spirits for the prisoners.   The Turks were much pleased with these presents, for they had not the slightest idea that they were only given as a blind, and therefore they encouraged the Greeks to bring alms for the poor prisoners still more frequently.   In both these casks were false bottoms, under which small hand-saws, files, silken cords, and all manner of instruments were stuffed ; and thus for more than a year the Greeks continued to come with their alms.   At last they paid a sum of money that the Turks might allow them to give all the prisoners linen for shirts.   The two prisoners managed so circumspectly with their correspondence, that not only the Turkish guards, but even their fellow-prisoners found nothing out, for these Greeks were very cunning people.   Thus, there was no one who had the least inkling that anybody was about to make his way and escape out of the tower.

When the Greeks had everything requisite ready to their hands, last of all two more casks with schnapps were brought to them, and then first it was that these two Greeks disclosed their views to the other prisoners, informing them that, with God's aid, they would help both the rest and themselves out of the prison.   But before they put their project into execution they were all obliged to kneel down, place two fingers upon the Gospel, and swear to keep the secret, and not to betray each other should their design be found out.   And then for the first time the prisoners were cheerful, and began to

L

make the guards tipsy with the schnapps, for the Turks are very fond of schnapps, which the Greeks make of excellent quality from figs and raisins.

One evening, when the guards were intoxicated, the two Greeks sawed in twain the rivets by which their own fetters and those of all the other prisoners were fastened, and soldered them together again with lead, in order that, if anybody should chance to look over them, he might find the fetters entire, and they might afterwards saw them through more easily in lead than iron, when need required. Every prisoner was also obliged to give the two Greeks his shirts, out of which they made a rope plaited throughout with the silken cord. On one occasion, then, they bade the rest of the prisoners to drink schnapps purposely with the Turkish guards, to sing, and to shout; meanwhile, messieurs the Greeks, during this shouting, cut through with the small saws the floors of the first, second, and third stories above them, so that a man could creep through, and through the third opening climbed to the window of the tower, whence they that night measured the height of the tower, and made the rope long enough to reach to the ground. They had, moreover, a certain understanding with their friends, in consequence of which a swift boat, with a lantern burning all night long, was stationed by the sea-shore, and waited for them. The light burned all night in the lantern, in order that these Greeks might see whither to direct themselves when they got out of prison.

The next night—for the will of God was surely therein manifest—being the day of St. John the Baptist, they made their guards tipsy again, and during their first slumber gave the files to their fellow-prisoners.

All, except a German named Hernstein, who only filed through the fetter on one of his feet, cut through the rivets in their fetters, and crept one after the other in the dark to the openings through the floors. Here the two Greeks, being experienced in these matters, and knowing how dear a thing freedom is, were afraid of their hurrying one over the other down the rope, and that somebody would fall down and betray the rest. They, therefore, made a list of all the rest, and, constructing a kind of chair of rugs and twisted rope, let them down in it by ages, the oldest first, and slid down last themselves, without the chair, like monkeys. Being now all together, they first fell on their knees and thanked the Lord God, and, as soon as they had all climbed out of the entrenchments, the Greeks took with them a Maltese knight, and bade adieu to the rest, and, after advising them to look to their own safety, though nobody knew whither to turn, hastened to their boat, and, making no delay, sailed off merrily in safety, whithersoever they would.

A Hungarian, Balak Dak Istvan, who had been, some years before, a lieutenant in the army at Erlau, being now advanced in age, and sick besides, was unable to climb to the top of the bastions, but remained lying on the spot. When morning dawned, and the summons to devotion was given by the Turkish priests, the Turks saw the rope hanging down from the tower, and quickly raised a shout. They then ran up into the tower, and saw the place through which all the prisoners had crept. The governor, all terrified, went immediately to Constantinople, and made known what had happened. All the gates in Constantinople and Galata were therefore shut, and many thousand people searched for the prisoners on all sides, by land and by water, but found none of them, except the Hungarian who was sitting in the fosse. Three days afterwards the German, Hernstein, was found among the vineyards, he not having been able to get rid of his fetters. When they were both brought before the chief pasha, and had given a true account of their escape, he asked the mufti, or chief priest, what he should do with the prisoners? The mufti immediately bade him not to do them any harm, but to remember that, although a bird in a cage has enough to eat and drink, yet, nevertheless, it seeks a hole through which to make its way out; much more does a prisoner, who suffers hunger, misery, and want, longing for freedom, as a reasonable creature, seek out all manner of means to set himself free; therefore those persons were not guilty, or deserving of any punishment, but their guards deserved to be punished capitally, since they had not done what their duty required, and had thoughtlessly let loose such important prisoners, who might be a cause of great damage to the Turks. The pasha, without delay, commanded all the guards who had had the watch that day, and their chief commanders, to be hung in the fortress, immediately appointed another aga, named Mehemet, and committed the two prisoners to his vigilance, with the advice to take warning from the fate of the previous governor, and, if he did not wish to lose his life as well, to look better to the guards himself.

Three months afterwards the Turks captured two other prisoners, Hungarians, who had also escaped at that time from the Black Tower, viz. Christopher, an innkeeper, and Matthew, a hussar. The own brothers

of this hussar,* who was a gallant knight of Hungary,
and had defended himself valiantly, killing many of the
Turks, had kept both these prisoners in Constantinople,
in the house of a Hungarian renegade, who bought them
a handsome horse each, and gave them clothes and
money to make their way to Hungary.   When they
rode, like soldiers, out of Galata, they had no knapsacks,
and therefore, to their misfortune, dismounted and
bought them in a shop.   Just then a servant of the aga
who had been hung happened to recognize the hussar
Matthew, and cried out, " This is the hussar Mathyas,
who got out of the Black Tower." The Turks, hearing
this, immediately ran after them by hundreds, and seized
them both.   They alleged, in their defence, that they
were Turkish hussars from Buda, bidding them leave
them alone, and saying that they had been to see after
their own affairs at court, and even naming the commander under whom they were serving, and appealing
to the aga of the janissaries.   And when they were
brought to him, they spoke so craftily before him, and
made out their case so well, that the aga rebuked the
Turks, and ordered them to let them go their way.

   Both these men had been captured in Hungary in
childhood, had been circumcised, and become Turks,
and had learnt the Turkish language well.   When they
grew up they returned to Christendom, forsook the
Mahometan error, and, being taken prisoners a second
time, were sent to the Black Tower.   When they were
just going to mount their horses again, a spahi, or
cavalry soldier, from the Black Sea, met them, immediately recognized them both perfectly, called them by

* It would seem that these brothers were renegades (?).

their names, and demanded that they should be watched by a guard, since he knew them as well as his own eye. They were, therefore, immediately seized, bound, and placed again in the Black Tower, where we afterwards found them, and shared their imprisonment. When we had already been half-a-year at the galleys, the Turks became fearful lest some of us should escape, and conducted us all back again from the galleys to our first prison, where they left us about a week.

Intelligence was again brought that our men had gained a glorious victory over the Turks in Hungary, whence great sorrow and lamentation arose on all sides; and the clerk of the prisoners, Alfonso di Strada, a Spaniard, who had gained his liberty by work and service, came to us early in the morning, and sorrowfully informed us that the Turks were violently enraged with us, and, in short, were on the point of putting us in the Black Tower, but that he did not in any wise wish us such a prison. Upon this we all fervently besought the Lord God that we might be released from that very terrible tower.

After dinner the pasha's kihaja ordered us to be all called out, and made known to us the will of his pasha, and also bade us take our things and follow him, saying that we were to sail to the Black Tower. As soon as we heard the Black Tower mentioned, and received the unhappy news that we were to be placed in so gloomy a prison, we all with one voice began to weep and lament, till our hearts were breaking. All the other prisoners pitied us too, and wept with us; moreover, we would rather have undergone death than go to so unendurable a prison. Having, therefore, tied up our things in wallets, and each taking his own property on his shoulders, we mournfully bade adieu to the prisoners, but were unable to speak for excessive weeping. All who were in the prison accompanied us with tears and lamentations to the gate.

A sad and sorrowful journey! indeed, the heart could then have broken with sorrow. One prisoner gave us half a loaf of bread as a parting gift, another some sewing needles, another a piece of cotton, and each what he had. When we came to the gate, and thus sorrow-fully weeping, thanked the Quardian Pasha of the place for having been kind to us, he too wept over us with compassion, and, intending to console us, said to us:— " Now, my dear prisoners, as the prophet Mahomet knows, I do not wish you that grievous prison, whence ye will never come forth till the day of your deaths, and will never meet your friends. I pity you, poor creatures! And yet, if ye be willing to become Turks, ye will be released from all this, and will receive special presents from the pasha.   My counsel is that ye do so, for when ye arrive there ye will be forgotten by all who knew you.   That prison is called the grave of the living, because the prisoners stay there, as in a grave, and never come out again."

These words of the pasha caused us still more pain and heartfelt sorrow, and after embracing each other we bade adieu to the prisoners and all the Turks.   At parting the Quardian Pasha ordered a loaf of bread with a draught of wine to be given each of us, but we could neither eat nor drink, nay, we could not even speak or see for weeping, knowing that we had no hope of getting out of that tower to the day of our death.

Truly, it was a great wonder that none of us died suddenly on the spot, for our hearts were broken with terror. Thus, getting into the boat, not with tears, but with great moaning, we looked sadly towards Constantinople, and seeing the column standing by our former house, gazed sorrowfully at it, reminding each other how we had previously had satisfaction and pleasure, but now were miserable prisoners in perpetual imprisonment. In truth, no man can sufficiently express our great misery and sorrow at that time; and now that I am writing this I cannot defend myself against anguish of heart, and therefore I will rather turn from the subject.

When we drew near the fortress where the Black Tower is, the Turks pointed it out to us, comforting us and bidding us have hope in God, saying that He was mighty and could release us from it, as indeed half-a-year before the prisoners had got out of it; but we could neither speak nor look for weeping and anguish, and it is wonderful where so many tears stow themselves away in the eyes. Had it not been for our souls we would rather have jumped into the sea and drowned ourselves, for excessive terror and panic had seized us, knowing that no hope remained of getting out of the tower. Nay, we knew that the new aga would wish to guard us more securely than the former prisoners had been guarded, as indeed turned out to be the case.

As soon as we ran ashore under the fortress itself a ladder was let down to us, up which, each carrying his wallet on his shoulders, we walked into the fortress after our reis, or captain. On approaching the great iron gates, which were opened to us, we saw a square with a gallery round it reaching to the tower itself, which was

entered by an iron door. The captain of our boat
handed to Mehemet, the aga, or governor, of the Black
Tower, a letter from the chief pasha, on perusing which
the aga said with a loud voice :—" What am I to do with
these poor prisoners? They have not deserved so severe
a prison. Is there no less severe prison to be found for
them? It is not just to punish guiltless people thus."
And looking at us, for we were all weeping from the
bottom of our hearts, and had our eyes bloodshot from
weeping, he said:—" *Allah Biuckter, kurtulur Siue!*" *i. e.*
" Fear not, God is a mighty liberator." He then ordered
that terrible door to be opened, and bade us go into the
tower.

Now let every compassionate heart consider how great
was our lamentation, weeping, and wailing, when we had
no hope left of coming out again by that door to the
day of our death, except as corpses. Alas! greater
sorrow than this there is not! Where no hope more
remains one does not wish to live. We, therefore, desired to die a sudden death before entering the tower.
But all was in vain, for God would have it thus. When
we entered that frightful gloomy tower we found in
it the above-mentioned four prisoners, who welcomed
us sorrowfully, and had no wish for us to be their companions in misery and trouble. Where each seated himself, there he was obliged to sit, to lie, and to have his
miserable dwelling for more than two years.

The tower is very lofty, but not very wide, so that
two-and-twenty of us and the first four, that is, six-
and-twenty persons, could scarcely lie down alongside
of each other; and, indeed, could not help touching
each other. Inside the tower is a thick oaken lattice,

like a cage in which lions are kept, so conveniently constructed that the guards can walk inside round the lattice, within which the prisoners sit, and see what they
are doing. In the middle of this cage burns, day and
night, a glass lamp, and round are stumps, or blocks, on
which we supported our feet. We were, indeed, to
have had our feet fastened in these blocks, but, as it
pleased God to grant us to find favour in the eyes of the
governor, he did not put us into the blocks, except
when Turks whom he did not know were to come to
the tower, when he sent guards in first with orders to
put both our feet into the blocks and fasten us in. On
the departure of the Turks he used to order us to be let
out again.

This governor had been a Christian child, born in
Croatia, and was then more than ninety years old ; zealous in his religion, and compassionate towards us, but care-
ful in his duties. He looked to the guards himself, came
frequently into the tower, and had the fetters examined
every day. Every week the guards examined all our
clothes over the whole body, to see whether they could
find a knife or file on any one, and, taking warning from
the aga who had been hung, he did not allow his diligence
to relax in the least. Accordingly, the next morning he
ordered us all to be led one after the other out of the
tower, and large iron fetters to be clinched on the feet of
each, and then bade us return to the tower. The Lord
God then raised up for me a good friend among the guards,
a Croatian renegade, who advised me to go out of the
tower last. When all my comrades had been provided
with fetters on their feet, and had returned to the tower,
I was conducted before the aga and his councillors, just

as I was, in my shirt, and only having a torn upper garment over it. The Croat said to them, " There are no more fetters." The aga, on hearing this, commanded me to go into the tower without irons ; but his councillors would not allow it, explaining to him, that, young as I was, I might, nevertheless, help myself and the rest of my companions out of prison, and that he well knew himself what danger he would afterwards be in. They therefore agreed that I should be fettered, and, as they had no more fetters, they put two iron rings round each of my feet, and riveted them to a chain. Thus I, too, was constrained to drag myself back to the tower after my companions with tears.

When the third day came, and neither bread nor other food was given us, we sent for our aga, and asked what they wanted to do with us. And it being already the third day since we had had anything in our throats, if they wanted to kill us with hunger, we bade them throw us into the sea and drown us, that we might, at any rate, be quit of our misery. When we wept before him, he had such compassion on us that tears fell from his eyes, and he said to us :—" As God lives, and his great prophet Mahomet, I do not wish you so grievous and gloomy a prison ; and I cannot wonder sufficiently why they imprison you, and give no orders what is to be done with you further. I do not think that they are going to kill you with hunger, for surely they would not have put you among the other prisoners ; but you would have been put into a vault, where they kill the other Turks with hunger. Therefore, I will go immediately to Constantinople, and ascertain, and inform you directly, what is to happen with you further." All of us then kissed his hand, his clothes, and his feet, recommended ourselves to his care with tears, and waited in great terror for his arrival.

Returning before evening from Constantinople, he comforted us by telling us that they were not going to kill us, and declared that he had obtained orders to the effect that three aspers, or kreutzers, a-day should be given to us to live upon by the pasha, adding also as follows:— " Since ye still have to wait long for the payment, for the wages of court officials and soldiers are paid quarterly, and your pensions will be paid then, I must, therefore, provide you with means of support in the interval." And these he provided as follows. Knowing we could not wait for the money, like a good man, he made himself our surety to the bakers in the town by the Black Tower, arranging that they should give each of us two loaves of bread daily, and he would pay them the money every quarter. He also kept his promise, for at the conclusion of the quarter he paid the bakers, and kept for himself the third kreutzer *per diem* for his trouble, though certainly he said that they refused to give us more than two aspers, a sum which we were obliged to receive thankfully. And since the salt sea-water could not be drunk, they brought good water from a spring on a hill some *hons* from the town, and gave us two pitchers of it daily, so that, hot as it was in our prison, we could scarcely quench our thirst, and often quarrelled together for the water, when one drank more of it than another. Therefore, that there might be equality amongst us, we took up the stocking trade, and made partnerships of five or six persons in each—one spinning the cotton, another winding it together, a third knitting, and so forth. When we had earned some money by selling what we had knit (for sometimes they sent us for it meal, oil, bread, vinegar, and even some aspers), we all clubbed together and bought as many mugs as there were persons, and also a large wooden tub, in which we set our mugs, and when the water was brought we filled them one after the other, till we had all had our turn; but when there was any water remaining in the tub each took it for a day in turn, and kept it for himself in a large pitcher.

We bought ourselves, moreover, a large pot, and plastered it with clay, which our guards brought us, and made a kind of oven of it. We also bought coals and a bag with the proceeds of our knitting, and being already in partnership by fives and sixes, and having saved several pitchers of water, each had to boil and act in turn as cook for a week; that is to say, taking a small loaf and two or three pieces of bread, he crumbled them into the water, got up the fire, boiled the porridge, and gave it to his fellow-craftsmen to eat. The stockings and gloves which his partners knitted he had to wash out in warm water, when there happened to be a sufficiency of water, and to wring out the shirts, their owners, meanwhile, sitting naked, and also to wash their heads, and thus was manager for a whole week, and then gave up his office to another. The porridge was extremely nice, especially when at times we procured some olive oil, made it rich for ourselves, and licked our fingers afterwards. Sometimes we had bread in sufficiency, and sometimes we had to wait all day till the very evening; sometimes, when they saw that we had water by us, they brought us no fresh water for a day or two: and thus we lived at their mercy. We had nothing gratis but salt, of which several vaults under ground had been full ever since Sultan Mahomet besieged Constantinople, and provisioned this fortress. Of this salt the aga sent us plenty.

When we had got used to the frightful darkness, and had formed this arrangement together, we obtained some Latin and German books, that is to say, the · Bible, poems, and legends; and whenever our guards were changed we concluded that it was day, and all sang a morning hymn, and read a legend, praying to the Lord God for our release, and for the victory of the Christians over the Turks; after which each turned to his work and worked all day. In the evening, when they had examined our fetters, we again sang an evening hymn, and, after performing our devotions, concluded that it was night, and betook ourselves to repose, or read a brief hour by the light of the lamp. It was, indeed, a great comfort that we obtained those books, and read to each other in them.

The Turks certainly laughed at our singing and praying, but they offered us no hindrance therein, and when the time of their own devotions came they observed it also. We poor prisoners, seeing that it could not be helped, comforted each other, and having no other hope, unless it should come to a peace, committed ourselves in all respects to God, and patiently endured darkness, hunger, stench, and filth in abundance; for there was no other place for us to go to for easement except a large gutter, to which we were all obliged to go without exception, and wash away the filth with water. There arose thence a stench so great that sometimes it was an annoyance to the Turkish guards, and they held their noses

when they went round watching what we were doing,
and reviled us violently. We, however, took no more
notice of any stench, for we were already accustomed
to it, and only laughed at them. Alas! how memory
flew back to our own dear country! What promises
we made of how good we would be, if God should help
us back to our own nation! How often we wished to be
day-labourers with our friends, that we might only be
able to earn bread in sufficiency, and have enough to
eat! We also remembered our past splendour and
superfluities, lamenting and heartily bewailing that we
had so lightly valued the gifts of God. Desiring, also,
to know whether our parents and friends were still alive,
and being acquainted with a prisoner in Galata, who had
earned his freedom by work and service, we sent him,
by one of our guards, the stockings and gloves, purses
and Turkish hats, which we had knitted, as above described, to convert them into money for our use, adding,
moreover, secret letters, to be delivered at Prague by
way of Venice. In this matter he behaved faithfully,
and bought us provisions for the money which he gained,
and carefully sent the letters, so that they were delivered
at Prague. For instance, about three from me reached
the late Herr Adam von Hradetz, chief *burggraf* of Prague
my patron, who was pleased to assist me to go to
Turkey. In these letters some of us informed his grace
of our imprisonment, and of other Turkish matters of
the day, and begged for aid.

Wishing, also, to learn to speak and write Turkish,
that I might, some day, be able to serve my country by
my knowledge of that language, I began to learn to
read Turkish, and through diligent application, in two

months, I began almost to talk, and could already read. For a Turkish priest used to come to me in the prison and teach me, and I promised to give him some stockings and gloves for his trouble. My two partners also learnt with me. It was very surprising to the Turk that I comprehended their letters and language in so short a time, and he spread wonderful reports about me everywhere. When our old aga came to know this, he came into the tower, and I had to read to him. He also wondered at my attainments, and promised me that it would be well with me to the day of my death if I would become a Mussulman; for when Cykula Pasha, a born Italian, came to know of me, I should be compelled, *nolens volens,* to become a Turk. If, then, I wished to remain a Christian, I should leave off my studies. At this I was exceedingly terrified, and my companions, also, gave me similar advice. I satisfied the Turkish priest, and left off learning. May the Lord God recompense the aga for his counsel, for I really should have been taken out of the tower and placed in that pasha's suite. When we had already been more than four quarters of a year in this Black Tower, with only one shirt and one rug a-piece, the violent frosts and cold wet west-winds tormented us in winter, just as much as the great heat had done in summer, and therefore our aga made us each a coat of cloth, in which we clad ourselves and kept out the cold.

Being all emaciated with hunger, our guards begged for us, from the fishermen, a large fish, just like a round table, and with a long tail, which the Turks call a *kedy baluk,* or cat-fish. This fish is not eaten, but its fat, for it is very fat, is melted down. Our guards begged this

fish, which had been caught in the sea, from the fishermen, and when they gave it us we received it with
great gratitude, and asked them to cut it in pieces for
us. When they had done as we wished, we were off
with several pieces immediately to the pot, boiled some,
baked the rest, and breakfasted off it with remarkably
good appetites, though afterwards we paid for it bitterly.
For we ate this fish's fat, and drank water after it, till
our stomachs and bellies swelled, so that for many
weeks we did not rise from our places. I, and some of
the rest, feeling sure that it must be some poison, were
affected with violent sickness and diarrhœa, which lasted
several days, and thence arose a dysentery, which weak-
ened us so much that some of us could not move from
the place where we were, but were obliged to lie in our
own filth. The Turks laughed at us loudly, having put
the fish in our way on purpose. When, after this
sickness, dysentery, unbounded stench, and such a foul
vapour arose that the guards themselves could not endure it, we informed our aga that we were all seriously
ill, and that death awaited us. He came amongst us,
and, seeing us in this condition, vehemently reproached
the Turks, and threatened to punish them for poisoning
us. He also asked our doctor what kind of medicine
we ought to use. We begged for some garlic and a
draught of brandy, and, clubbing together, induced the
aga to allow us to buy a small cask of brandy. Then,
eating the garlic and drinking the brandy, we immediately felt benefited, and some of us recovered, but
others felt the effects as long as they remained in the
prison. Our aga, seeing that we were better, was glad,
and strictly forbad anything to be given us without his

M

knowledge; he also had the prison cleaned out, and some weeks afterwards fumigated with laurel-leaves. They, nevertheless, gave us snails and tortoises, which we boiled and ate with a good appetite. Neither did they do us any harm, for we had fortified our stomachs with hunger, and digested everything well, with the exception of that nasty cat-fish.

At that time there was a great plague in Thrace, and in almost all the islands beyond sea, so that in Constantinople itself, and its suburbs, about 80,000 people died in three months. In the town around our tower, which is called Genyhyssar, that is, New Castle, many people, and some of our guards, perished. There was great weeping and lamentation. The Turks, learning that there was a surgeon amongst us, sent and requested him to be let out of the tower. He had medicines prepared for them, and let blood by the middle vein of the arm, for he had still kept a lancet or so. Sometimes from twenty to thirty persons of both sexes came to him, and could not sufficiently wonder that our way of blood-letting caused so little pain; for the Turks pierce the vein with an Italian knife, and make a large hole, which cannot be done without considerable pain. And the surgeon began to be the best off amongst us, for they gave him plenty to eat, and sometimes sent him money, and, above all, he went into the dear open air and light of day, and refreshed himself,—a thing which we poor creatures could not enjoy, but must remain, day and night, in that dark and stinking tower.

When the bad weather changed, Synan Pasha won a victory in Hungary with the Turkish army. The Turks, therefore, fired thrice from all their artillery, both in

Constantinople, on board the war-boats, and even on the surrounding islands, and about twenty guns from our tower. This firing surprised us, and, not knowing what it meant, we inquired, and received for answer that the mighty Synan Pasha had taken from the Christians the fortress of Wanek, or Raab, the key of Christendom, the strongest fortress in the land of Hungary, which we were in no wise willing to believe.

After a week came fifteen Turks of rank, distinguished heroes, from Anatolia, on their return back from Hungary, and wished to speak with us. Our aga made haste and ordered us to be fastened to the blocks by both feet, and came to us with them.   They asked us whether we knew that Raab was taken? and whether any of us had been there?   When we answered that we had, and would not believe that it was lost, but asked how they got possession of it, they replied:—" You dogs, they say, do everything for money; and what a fool your king is to entrust such an impregnable fortress to that little count, who, being led by avarice, sold so important a fortress to Synan Pasha for a sum of money, and evacuated it; whereas we could not have taken it had we lain before it two years without intermission.   And thus it is that you Christian dogs build and fortify all your forts for us, for, as soon as we march up to them, we get possession of them either by force or for money."

After this they told us how much artillery, provisions, and booty of all kinds they found in Raab. We were at last obliged to believe, with sorrow, that Raab was lost. These Turks brought us a basket of bread, divided it amongst us, and encouraged us to trust in God, for He was able to deliver us even out of that grievous prison.

They, too, they said, as soldiers, must expect a similar
misfortune to that which had befallen us, adding:—
" *Bwgium sise, jarambise;* " " To-day to you, to-
morrow to us;" " for," said they, " it is destined for
each what fate he is to meet with." When they saw
us chained in fetters, and, moreover, with our feet in
the blocks, they had compassion on us, and spoke to the
aga not to treat us so harshly.   For, just as with us no
sensible people insult the Jews, but the mob, when they
meet one, give him a fillip, or a kick, or knock his hat
off his head, so also no respectable Turks insult the
Christians much, but only the worthless mob, who will
not be subject to any order or law.

When Synan Pasha returned from Hungary, and delivered the silver key from the fortress of Raab to his
Sultan, Amurath, he was received and welcomed with
great and inexpressible glory, so that nothing was talked
about for a long time but his valour; and the vulgar
Turks imagined that there were no more fortresses in
Christendom, but Vienna and Prague.   Our guards,
too, advised us to turn Turks, if we wished to be released from prison, assuring us that, when spring came,
the Sultan himself would go to Hungary, and take
Vienna and Prague; and whither should we betake
ourselves?   But we gave them far different information
about Christendom, at which they wondered greatly,
and would not believe us, because they were otherwise
instructed by their popaslars, or priests.

All that winter the Turks made preparations for a
campaign in Hungary, and said that with the spring the
Emperor himself would march, which both I, and the
priest, John von Winor, my countryman and fellow-

prisoner, made known to our friends at Prague, by way
of Venice. As soon as spring came news arrived of the
victory of the Prince of Transylvania over the Turks
and Tartars, and Synan Pasha, having been fortunate
with Raab, was proclaimed generalissimo of the army
in the field. Fresh soldiers and janissaries were added
to the old ones, and Synan promised to bring the land
of Transylvania finally under the power of the Sultan;
and, in fact, the Turks told us that he was every day
expected to march out of the city with a very fine army
of 80,000 men. The longer they waited, the more it
was noised abroad about Transylvania, and how our
people were strengthening themselves on both sides;
and Synan Pasha rode most magnificently out of Constantinople, and waited a week before the city till the
whole army assembled. Ibrahim Pasha remained as
governor of the city in his place.

At that juncture no small alteration took place in
Turkey. Some people in Asia thought fit to be insub-
ordinate, but Ibrahim Pasha ordered them to be arrested,
and put in prison in our tower above us. He also
ordered people to go slyly and put a Georgian lord
in prison with us. He was a well-made, tall young
fellow. These distinguished Turks were taken, about
midnight, from prison down to the sea, and thrown in.
And when one was thrown into the sea a cannon was
fired on our tower, at which we were greatly terrified,
especially as, when each Turk was led away to be
drowned, we heard how the poor man lamented and
prayed. Thus they dealt with them several nights in
succession, till they had drowned them all; and they
threatened us that we should be treated in the same

way.   Almost at the same time several of the principal pashas died suddenly, as well as Sultan Amurath himself.   Some said that boils burst out on his thigh, from which he died.   His death was concealed until his son, Mehemet, came from Amazya to Constantinople ; otherwise, if the soldiers had known of his death, they would have plundered the whole city, Jews and Christians. For it is a custom with them that, when the Sultan dies, the soldiers have licence to plunder the merchants.

When, therefore, Sultan Mehemet arrived incognito, his nineteen brothers were immediately strangled with a cord by mutes, who are always employed for that purpose.   One of these brothers begged hard to be only allowed to look his brother in the face, but the poor man was unable to obtain this favour.   Two wives of the preceding Sultan, who were pregnant, were also thrown into the sea ; and afterwards all who were thus strangled were shown to the Emperor, lying on splendid carpets, when he ordered them to be put into coffins and buried very expensively and magnificently, in the chapel with their father, and a turban, with a handsome plume of cranes' feathers, to be placed on the head of each.   He then took complete possession of his rights, renewed the offices of some, and dismissed others from their posts.

On one occasion Ibrahim Pasha, who had married a daughter of the new Sultan, went on an excursion to a delightful garden which he owned by the Black Sea, beyond our tower.   Our old aga obtained intelligence of this, and came amongst us and told us that Ibrahim, who had been well disposed towards our ambassador, was going to his gardens, and, therefore, counselled us, whenever a salute should be fired from the two fortresses,

that is, from the cannon on our tower and the castle
opposite, to raise our voices and wish the pasha prosperity, and all that was good, promising, also, to intercede for us with him, for which we returned him many
thanks. As soon as they began to fire, we shouted with
the utmost power of our throats, wishing prosperity to
the pasha; and our aga, going in a small boat to the
pasha, as he sailed past our fortress, informed him of our
great necessity; and Ibrahim asked who and what
manner of prisoners we were, and, on hearing that we
were servants of the late imperial ambassador, ordered
him to bring a couple of us to him in the garden. The
aga landed and came to us immediately with joy, and,
informing us of the pasha's order, asked us whom we
wished to send him. On hearing this, and having all
kissed the hem of his garments, we deputed the priest,
John von Winor, and the doctor of medicine, an old
man about sixty years of age, who had long grey hair
flowing over his shoulders. These our deputies had
scarcely any shirts, but lice, insects, and other filth in
abundance; and when they issued forth out of such darkness, it was impossible for them to gaze at the brightness
of the sun, for, their eyes being disused to the light,
tear followed tear, so that they were like blind men.
Then our aga—Ibrahim being by birth a Croatian—
told the priest, John, how and what to say to him, and
bade them both fall at his feet, kiss them, and entreat
for our release. As these our deputies could not see,
he led them like blind men on board the boat, into which
the aga also entered with them, and they sailed to the
pasha's garden. On getting out of the boat they espied
Ibrahim leaning on two young men, and walking about

in the garden. On seeing them in such miserable plight, just like corpses that had risen from the grave, very pale, emaciated, and nothing but skin and bones, he stood still, and they, being led up to him, fell at his feet, and our aga, indignant at their misery, did not wait for the priest to make his speech to the pasha, but spoke for them himself, saying :— " Lo, here, gracious lord, thou hast these people, who came to us on an embassy, and in silver, in brocade, and in velvet clothing, brought presents of honour to my lord our Emperor, as thou thyself also sawest formerly! Behold, what a change has come to the unfortunates! Are they like living men or dead? Our most holy Alcoran doth not teach us thus to torture guiltless ambassadors. It is now approaching the third year since they have been in this unendurable prison, in irons and fetters, in darkness, with bread and water scantily supplied for nourishment. Have compassion on them for the recompence of the prophet Mahomet! Nay, we shall never enjoy any prosperity so long as we torture and torment with imprisonment these guiltless persons. Look on these unfortunates! See! they are nothing but shadows, and these are stronger than any of the rest."

Ibrahim replied :—" Dear aga, thou knowest that I am not grand vizier, but am only his lieutenant for the time. Since the mighty Synan Pasha commanded them to be put in prison, God forbid that I should undertake anything counter to him! But when he returns in health, I will make sufficient intercession to him, that they may be quit of so grievous an imprisonment; and, if I were grand vizier myself, I would set them free immediately without deliberation." Then, taking eight ducats out of a bag, he gave them to our two deputies, to be divided amongst us. Our deputies thanked him for his present and condescension, and departed. Our aga then ordered the ducats to be changed and divided amongst us, whence forty kreutzers, or aspers, fell to the share of each. Then, for the first time, we feasted, and bought ourselves as much bread, meal for porridge, oil, meat baked in the sun, and other provisions as we wanted, thanking the Lord God and the pasha for such a benefaction.

Our aga thenceforth comforted us, saying that, when once Synan came from Transylvania, we should have a good friend in Ibrahim, and that he would release us from this grievous prison. On one occasion he asked us, if it pleased God to help us out of prison, what would we give him in return, for we knew that he was our good friend, and he promised to be so still more? We alleged in excuse our pennilessness and poverty, and when we promised him that, as we had no money, we would give him everything that we had, and what we knitted besides, he laughed at us, admitted that he did not want our rags, but wished to know whether, in order that he might look the better after our affairs with the pasha, we were willing to secure him 500 ducats in the hands of the Christian merchants, and give them to him for his trouble if he should help us out of prison? Longing for freedom, we promised to give him 200 ducats, imagining that we could easily provide such a sum as that among the merchants; and thus our aga journeyed so much the oftener to Constantinople, and spoke of us in Ibrahim's presence.

On one occasion Ibrahim invited the Sultan to his

gardens, on learning which our aga came to us, shouting :
—" Good news, Christians! good news! The most mighty
Sultan makes an excursion to-morrow to Ibrahim's gardens. Therefore, when a cannon is fired on the tower,
shout with all the voice you have, and wish the Emperor
prosperity and victory over his enemies." We heard this
with great joy, kissed his hands and clothes, and thanked
him for the advice. In the morning the Sultan issued
magnificently from his palace, with the firing of heavy
artillery, with shouting, and wishing of prosperity, on
the part of all the people who stood in order on the shore,
with their heads bent down to their knees, but stopped
on meeting his monks, or hermits, who lived a mile* from
Constantinople, and deliberated with them about all manner of things for two hours. These monks, as we afterwards heard, counselled him, since much Mussulman blood
had been shed in Hungary, to appease the prophet Mahomet by almsgiving, and, if he had any prisoners who
were innocent, or had earned their freedom by work and
service, to release and set them at liberty. After this
advice he took leave of them, and sailed along the shore
past the tower in which we were, in a boat gilded all over,
as our guards told us. The Turks fired heavy artillery
in honour of him, and our aga, with everybody from the
town welcomed him, with their hands crossed and with
great humility, and bending their heads to the ground,
shouted with a loud voice :—" God preserve thee and thy
Majesty in health for ever!"

As soon as they ceased firing, we all called out and
shouted with a loud voice, wishing him prosperity, our

* A Latin mile is nearly equal to an English mile. A German
mile is rather more than four English miles.

guards also assisting us in so doing. The Emperor heard
the noise, but could not understand anything. When
the Emperor sailed gently on, and the shouting increased
more and more the farther he went, he asked what the
noise was, and whence it came. Then the Lord God raised
up a friend for us, Bostangi Pasha, the grand superintendent of the gardens, who stood behind the Emperor, and
commanded the guard in the stern of the boat, and he
said to the Emperor :—" This voice, most gracious Emperor, is that of poor prisoners, who have now been long
in yon tower, and see not the light of the sun ; they are
calling and begging for mercy." The Emperor stopped,
and asked what manner of prisoners they were? Information was given him that they were the servants of the
ambassador of the Viennese king, who had been sent to
his father, Sultan Amurath, with the annual gift and
handsome presents, and that their lord had been a traitor,
and had written down all manner of intelligence for his
king ; also that Synan Pasha had commanded him to be
put to death in prison, and his suite to be placed in that
tower, and that, though guiltless, they had already been
three years imprisoned in irons.

Upon this the Emperor said :—" Since they are guiltless prisoners, and have never drawn the sword against us,
it is not a proper thing to afflict them by imprisonment;
therefore, I command that they be released." He then
went on his way. Then the kind Turks and guards
who heard this ran tumbling over each other to us,
hoping to receive presents for telling us some very good
news. And when we promised them, they informed us
that their Emperor had given orders to set us at liberty.
Then, being filled with boundless joy, we distributed to

them everything that we had, rugs, clothes, and spirits, and kissed and embraced each other, not imagining but that we should be set free in the morning. But we were shamefully deceived. For there in heathendom, just as with us Christians, when the Emperor makes any promise to any one, if that person has not a good friend at court, and if he makes no presents, his just matter is often left in the lurch. Thus it happened to us poor wretches. For having given away everything that we possessed, we had afterwards to suffer hunger and all manner of want; and whereas we might have lain on the rugs, we were obliged to be satisfied with the bare ground.

At this time a German, a goldsmith in Galata, who had assisted Herr von Hofkirch and many other prisoners in getting out of prison, had it proved against him, and was put in gaol, and tortured, and before daybreak the poor fellow was thrown on a hook. When the Turks searched his house, they found copies of intelligence which he had been in the habit of sending by letter to Christendom, and immediately put many Christian merchants in prison on mere suspicion; but let them out again, when the unfortunate man made no confession to implicate them. The Emperor's mother was very fond of this goldsmith, for he was a very good craftsman, and used to do all that she wanted. As soon as she heard that he was arrested, she immediately ordered him to be released; but before the order arrived the poor man had been hung upon the hook. It was a pity. He was a very good man, and assisted many Christian prisoners to freedom. May it please the Lord God that his soul may come into the number of the elect!

News now arrived that Synan Pasha was returning

to Constantinople with a small number of soldiers, and on this account there was great clamour, weeping, and wailing. Moreover, some of the pashas, who envied Synan his prosperity, were glad, and brought him into disfavour with the Emperor, so that the Emperor made him mazul, and forbad him to ride to court under penalty of death. For "having," as it was said, "purposely lost so many distinguished youths, he was not worthy to receive honour and thanks, but deserved rather to be strangled." He was, therefore, commanded not to come into the Emperor's sight, but to remain on his own estate, and not to quit it without the Emperor's leave. Thus he was in great disfavour, so that the Turks began to say that he would eventually be strangled—a fate which we heartily wished him. Synan, being an old, cunning, and experienced fox, took an insult like this very much to heart, and by a written petition entreated to be allowed to prove his innocence, and be heard as well as his adversaries; but the chief pashas conspired against him, and would not allow his petition to come before the Sultan.

Understanding this, he obtained his wish by great presents. That is to say, he sent fifty mules' burthen of gold, silver, precious stones, carpets, and other valuable things, which were appraised altogether at 100,000 ducats, to the Emperor's wife and mother, and ordered them to be told that he had brought all this for them from Hungary. Through this cunning, and the value of his gifts, he was admitted to the Emperor's presence before he expected. He kissed his hand, wished him good fortune and prosperity in a long reign, and then, as the Turks said, made a speech to the Emperor to the following effect:—
" Mighty Emperor! my heart pains me in my old and

already decayed body that I am so monstrously calum-
niated before thee, and brought into disgrace, because
this year fortune has to some extent been adverse to me,
and I have lost some soldiers in battle, whereas it is impossible that fortune should remain constantly on one
side.   I greatly pity thy youth, because thou hast not
upright counsellors, and because as soon as any man gives
thee intelligence thou believest him, whereas one ought
first to inquire sufficiently, whether it be so.   I served
thy great grandfather, grandsire, and father, even to these
grey hairs; I have aided thy house to conquer many
kingdoms and countries; I have shed much of my blood
for the extension of thy dominions.   I conquered Tunis,
Golleta, Famagusta, and last year the fortress of Wanek,
or Raab, the key of all Christendom, so that, if thou desirest, thou hast an easy access to Vienna, and to all the
empire, whereas, neither thy grandsire, nor thy father,
ever took so famous a fortress.   And now, whereas thou
oughtest to give me thanks for this, since I have accom-
plished more than all the pashas, I have, on the contrary,
been brought into disgrace with thee, and it has been
forbidden me to gaze at thy Majesty and serve at court.
Although, being experienced as well in home as in
foreign affairs, having spent my youthful years in the
service of the Emperors, thy predecessors, and being now
more than ninety years old, I have it in my power to be
much more valuable to thee in council, and to serve thee
better, than all the present pashas, who are new and
young.   It was not thus that thy predecessors did; they
did not drive old councillors and experienced soldiers
from court, and regulate themselves by the advice of
young know-nothings."

After having said this, he began to relate the great irregularities of some of the pashas, and thereby brought his matter so far that he was again received into favour, and certain pashas dismissed from their posts. Ferhat Pasha was strangled the next day, and out of his property the Emperor ordered more than a million and a-half to be taken for his treasury.   Synan was made vizier, or chief over the pashas, in his place.

After this our allowance of two aspers each was not paid for a whole quarter, and our aga went to court and mentioned us to the vizier, who answered angrily that he would have us flayed alive, and our skins made into drums.   This was told us sorrowfully by the aga, who bade us entreat God that the vizier's anger might be appeased.   Then both our men and the Transylvanians took some fortresses from the Turks, and slew a good many. When this news was brought to Constantinople, the Turks immediately prepared for war, and Synan was proclaimed grand serdar, or commander-in-chief.

And since he had been very unfortunate in the preceding year, he used every exertion to prevail upon the Sultan to march into Hungary in person.   He also induced the soldiers, especially the spahis and janissaries, to make themselves heard, and declare that, since they had had no luck against the giaours under any pasha, they would not march to war without the presence of the Sultan; but, if he would go with them, every man, who had but the strength to do so, would march without opposition and with a good will. And not only did they make themselves heard orally to this effect; but when the Sultan went to church they presented him written petitions, requesting him to go to Hungary against the

Christians, and follow in the footsteps of his predecessors. But the Empress set herself in opposition to this,
relying upon the Alcoran, which ordains that no new
sultan, when he ascends the imperial throne, shall be
obliged to go to war for the space of three years. She,
therefore, bade Synan and the soldiers to be content,
counselling rather that Synan, and other old experienced
commanders, should march into Hungary. It was their
duty, she said, to protect their lord and his land ; indeed,
what good would their office be if they could not slay
the giaours without the Sultan's presence ? In that case,
did they deserve the dignity with which they were for
that purpose invested by the Sultan ? When, through
the urgency of Synan, the then vizier, and the soldiers,
the Emperor was inclined to go to Hungary, the vizier
immediately had all manner of military engines prepared,
everything requisite for an imperial campaign got ready,
and the soldiers mustered. But, through the great exertions he made for these purposes, a dysentery suddenly
attacked him so violently that he was constrained to
keep his bed. It was said that the Sultana corrupted
Synan the vizier's physician by bribes and splendid presents, so that he had something administered to him, and
died in eight days. Great lamentation was made by
the people for his death ; they wore mourning for him,
gave alms for the benefit of his soul, buried him with
great magnificence and veneration ; composed mournful
songs about his heroic deeds, and sang that the light of
valour and heroism was extinguished. Indeed, he was
truly a man of remarkable experience, and no one in
Turkey, at that time, could compare with him.

Our old aga came amongst us and informed us of his

death, with tears streaming from his eyes, and said:—
" It is news good for you, but mournful for us, that the
most experienced soldier and pillar of the Turkish dominions, Synan Pasha, is dead, who served our imperial
house faithfully, and often troubled the giaours, and
before whom no fortress could stand, which he did but
undertake to capture. 'Tis a pity, 'tis a pity, that that
experienced man is gone! But now that it has pleased
God, and the prophet Mahomet, that it should be so,
may his soul shine as the sun! Neither I, nor my
children, expect to see such a man again. Therefore,
I advise and expect you to pray to God that Ibrahim
Pasha, who sent you the alms, may be chosen grand
vizier in his room."

More than a fortnight passed while intrigues for that
office were going on, till, at last, Ibrahim Pasha was
chosen. At that time we were all heartily weary in the
tower, for we had been fettered in irons for three years
without intermission. Indeed, we often prayed with
tears, and besought God for release, especially when
very cold and disagreeable north-winds blew, till many
of us fell sick; on some of us the skin sloughed from
filth; others broke out into eruptions, and so great a
stench came from them, that not only was it offensive to
us, but even our guards were annoyed by such a smell.
They, therefore, brought us laurel-leaves, which we put
on the coals, like juniper, and fumigated with them, for
they grow them in abundance. And, in sooth, we longed
to die, being utterly enfeebled by hunger, and tortured
by that intolerable darkness and stench, for we had no
other hope of getting out of it, unless peace were made
between our Emperor and the Sultan. Rightly is that

Black Tower called " the grave of the living," for all
our friends and enemies alike forgot us, giving us no
assistance in any wise.   Yet many hundred ducats had
been sent, through a bill-of-exchange, both to me, to the
late Zahradetzky, and to the priest John von Winor;
but firstly, on account of the length and danger of the
journey, and secondly, on account of the strictness and
cruelty of our imprisonment, they could not be delivered
to us.   For, out of four thousand two hundred ducats,
I only got one hundred and fifty, and these I was obliged to give away, mention of which will be made below.
But verily the Holy Scripture is true, that, when all
human aid fails, GOD Himself succoureth with His
assistance.

BOOK IV.

Of our Release from Prison and Return to our own Country.

HILE we were thus mournfully lamenting and singing sad songs, and had lost all hope of quitting the tower till death, in comes our aga amongst us, with a cheerful countenance, bidding us give him a reward, because he was about to tell us good news. Waking up, as it were from sleep, we all crowded round him, like chickens round a hen, beseeching him to tell us the good news, kissing his feet, hands, and clothes. Not having the heart to refuse our request, he informed us that Ibrahim Pasha was chosen grand vizier, and gave us good hope of our release. On hearing this, without having had any expectation of it, we raised our hands and thanked God heartily, and asked the aga to advise us what we should do, for we scarce knew what to do for joy. For in truth, if a man has not experienced misery, want, hunger, cold, heat, and grievous imprisonment, he cannot possibly believe one who has been in such a condition. He advised us to send a petition to the pasha, and wish him prosperity in his new office, long life, and victory over his enemies, promising to deliver the petition to the pasha and to intercede for us ; but on condition that, on our release, we should give him the two hundred ducats. In return for this we kissed his hands and feet for joy, and promised to give him much more ; and having given the writing to a Turkish priest to copy out, we sent it to the aga to look over, committing ourselves to the Lord God and to him. He got into his caïque, or six-oared boat, and going to Constantinople, first wished Ibrahim joy of his new office, and then delivering the writing from us, spoke to the following effect: —" Call to thy recollection, gracious sir, that when thou wentest to thy gardens thou promisedst the prisoners in the Black Tower to befriend them and care for their release. But because thou wert then only a lieutenant in thy present dignity, these poor prisoners prayed for thee, day and night, that thou mightest become grand vizier, and never lay down to rest without singing a hymn to God for thee, according to their religion. Therefore, have compassion on the poor wretches ; though they are unbelieving dogs, nevertheless they are also God's creatures. Who knows, whether God has not heard them, and called thee to this office for their release ? For when I told them that thou wast proclaimed vizier, they all with tears and joy raised their hands towards heaven, and gave God thanks. And, moreover, the mighty Sultan himself commanded them to be released from prison. Therefore, they now place all their hope in thee and none other ; if thou wilt, free them from so grievous an imprisonment; and since they are innocent, thou wilt receive a recompence from Mahomet."

The pasha received our letter and said:—" Dear aga, thou perceivest and knowest how great a burden is placed upon me, so that I have more cares than hairs in my beard. Therefore, it is impossible to attend to them before I set more important matters in order. Remind me in about two or three weeks' time, and conduct them to the divan (the national council), and I will use every means that they may be freed from this imprisonment."

When the aga made this known to us we were filled with great joy, and waited anxiously for the time to come; and certain it is that those two weeks seemed to us as long a space as the four years preceding; for we were constantly thinking, whether the time was already come when we should be released from our prison. For such thoughts we could not even sleep. When the longed-for time came, the aga gave orders for us all to be let out of the tower, and the fetters to be taken off one foot. These we tied to our girdles, that we might carry them the more easily. On coming into the open air we were refreshed, as if born anew ; yet we could not look at the sun, but, on coming suddenly out of such great darkness into the light, tears streamed from our eyes, till they became accustomed to it again. Meanwhile the aga ordered the caïque to be prepared for us to sail to Constantinople; and on looking over us, and seeing me, the youngest of all, with long hair and no beard, pale and emaciated, he said that I should stay there below with the guards and walk about, till he returned with my comrades, otherwise, on account of my youth, I might easily be seized by some pasha and forced to turn Mahometan. For the Turks, and especially the renegades, are addicted to infamous crimes, and young people are in great danger.

He, therefore, honestly advised me to stay there. Wishing with my whole heart to make the excursion and see
Constantinople, I kissed the aga's hand, and besought
him, for God's sake, to take me also with him. He said
to me :—"If thou wilt have it so, thou shalt come with
us ; but I do not promise thee that thou wilt return."
Thus we got into the boat and sailed to Constantinople,
landed from the boat, and went into the city, where a
great concourse of the Turkish mob surrounded us, asking who and whence we were ? But our aga answered
them himself, and forbad us to say a word. Having
very long hair flowing over my shoulders, and being
beardless, I was the most tormented ; for one pulled me by
the hair, another stared in my face, a third talked to me,
and asked me who I was ; but the aga seeing this, and fearing for me, did not venture to take me into the divan :
but going to the church of St. Sophia, left me there
with two Turks, under a projection of the roof, where
some lime was lying, and ordered me to sit down on the
ground, that the Turks going that way might not see
me. He, likewise, ordered my two guards to give heed
to me, otherwise, as Cykula Pasha, an Italian renegade,
had gone to the council that day, I should certainly fall
into some danger if I went with the rest to the council.
Though unwillingly, I nevertheless remained there, and
the aga's idea was not far wrong. For, as soon as my
companions entered the divan, Cykula Pasha asked :—
" Where is the Viennese ambassador's boy, that he is not
with these ?" The aga answered :—" He has been seriously ill for several weeks, and I know not whether he will
be still alive when we return ; moreover, he is covered
with such an eruption that it is painful to look at him."

All the pashas present arose, went to the Sultan, and made intercession that we might be released from prison, saying that peace would be made between the Emperors so much the sooner. But orders were given to our aga to place us again in the tower, and bring me also if I were still alive, to the divan in a fortnight. The prisoners, my comrades, thanked the pashas, and returned towards the Black Tower, past the church of St. Sophia, where I sat in the lime-vault. I crawled out of the lime-vault and joined them with my two guards, and we went to the tower, and anxiously waited for the last day of the fortnight.

When the Emperor Mehemet came to the determination of besieging the city of Erlau in person, and all military matters were prepared, the embassies of the King of France and the Queen of England made intercession with Ibrahim Pasha for our release, promising, by means of us, to bring it to pass that peace should be made between the Sultan and the Emperor; for at that time the Turks were already weary of the war, and would rather have had peace than war, as the flower of their army had perished in Hungary.

After a fortnight we all sailed again to Constantinople with one fetter. On going into the divan we were informed, through an interpreter, that the mighty Sultan, out of his natural goodness, released us all from so grievous an imprisonment, and counselled us to show gratitude in return, and never to wage war against him; otherwise, if any of us were seized and captured in war, he would be immediately impaled. Likewise, when we returned to our own country, he bade us, with the aid of our friends, bring it to pass that our king should seek peace from the mighty Sultan, and that the prisoners on both sides should be released. Upon this they inscribed us by name in the record books, and all of us, falling at the feet of the pashas, wished to kiss them, which, however, they did not permit, and, thanking them for their great kindness, promised that none of us (knowing their great power and might) would serve in war to the day of our death ; but that, as soon as we arrived in Christendom, we would in every wise counsel our Emperor and our friends to humble themselves to the Sultan, and seek peace from him, and that we knew that negotiations for peace would be begun as soon as we informed them of such enormous preparations.

There were also there present the ambassadors of the King of France and the Queen of England, who were to follow the Turkish army to the city of Erlau, and to whom several camels and horses had been assigned, and also a chiaous appointed, with twenty janissaries, to protect them and prevent the Turkish multitude from injuring them in aught. These ambassadors befriended us, and entreated that we might be freed from prison immediately, and sent to Christendom by sea, by way of Venice. That request being made, the ambassadors and we were commanded to leave the council, and, after a short time, the pashas summoned the English ambassador, and bade him, whenever he should follow the Sultan, to take us under his protection, and provide for us, as far as Greek Belgrade. They then assigned us thirty-five camels and four carriages, to put our baggage on, and also ride on ourselves; and also promised to give us five tents and six janissaries for our safety, and meanwhile commanded us to depart to the tower, take

our necessaries (*i. e.* our rags), and wait upon the English ambassador.

It is impossible to express with what joy we returned
back to the tower, for we forgot all our miseries and
past troubles, thanked the Lord God heartily for this
kindness, and rejoiced just as if we had been born again.
As we drew near the Black Tower, the aga reminded
us in the boat of the promise we had made him, viz. our
engagement to give him 200 ducats. He immediately
sent some of our number, with one fetter on, to Galata,
to try to borrow the money amongst the Christian merchants. But they returned again to the tower without
having been able to effect anything, by great entreaties,
with any one who would take compassion on our misery,
and lend us the 200 ducats, and told the aga that they
had been unable to make arrangements anywhere. On
hearing this, he was greatly enraged, imagining that we
were able to obtain money, but were purposely endeavouring to avoid giving him anything. He, therefore, reproached us with threats, and angrily reminded us
of the kindnesses he had done us in the prison, calling
us ungrateful dogs and giaours, and swearing, by his
Sultan's head, that no one should make him release us
from prison till we paid him the 200 ducats according
to agreement. He then ordered the fetters to be fastened
again on both our feet, and commanded us to go into
the tower, and even into the stocks. We pacified him
with tears, and affirmed with great oaths that we really
could not make arrangements for such a sum, and begged
him, nevertheless, to send some more of us on the morrow out among the merchants, to see whether we should
be any more fortunate than we had been that day.

The next day, early in the morning, I and three others of knightly rank, and also the priest John, and our doctor, were released from our fetters, and sailed to Galata, where we negotiated with all the merchants, especially the Venetians, who were the most numerous, and endeavoured to prevail upon them to lend us 200 ducats. We were willing to subscribe with our blood that we would send them the money to Venice in half-a-year, and fifty ducats besides, by means of a bill-of-exchange, begging them, for God's sake, and for the sake of the recompence they would obtain, to take a Christian compassion upon our long imprisonment, to collect that sum amongst them, and assist us poor tortured prisoners with a loan. But not a spark of Christian love was there in them. Not only did they refuse to lend us the 200 ducats, but they would not even speak friendly with us, take compassion on our misery and sympathize with us; nay more, they avoided us, and said that they dared not talk with us for fear of suspicion. Then we went to the Venetian ambassador himself, told him who we were, and in what station our friends in Christendom were, begged him for a loan, and promised that we would repay the money to the Venetian ambassador at Prague, if he wished, with interest, and would bind ourselves to do so in writing. But we effected nothing more with him than with the rest of the merchants; he strangely alleged his poverty in excuse, and said that he had no ready money by him, but daily expected a large sum from his lords. Not knowing whither to betake ourselves, we went, last of all, to the French and English ambassadors, and informed them what an impediment to our liberation had arisen from the aga, begging them, for God and His mercy's sake, to take compassion upon us and lend us the money. But they, too, excused themselves on account of their great expenses, since they were about to follow the Sultan's camp, and were obliged to borrow from others themselves. However, they declared themselves willing to go thus far, viz. if the aga would take either cloth, or velvet, or house-furniture, they would send him articles in moderation to the value of the 200 ducats. With this answer they dismissed us.

Thus we, poor harassed creatures, returned to our tower with empty hands, great terror, weeping, and anxiety, and informed the aga that no one would lend us aught in ready money, unless he were willing to receive it in articles of commerce. On hearing this, he shook his stick at us, and threatened to beat us, if the Turks sitting by had not prevented him, called us liars in our throats, promise-breakers, and unfaithful dogs; recounted the acts of kindness which he had done us, and would not believe that we could not make arrangements about the money. " For," said he, " how can you but lie in your throats in saying that your Christians and brethren, of whom there are thousands, will not redeem you, whereas, if they gave an asper apiece, it would amount to a much larger sum than these 200 ducats? But the fact is, you dogs want to cheat me; you will not exert yourselves to obtain the money, but are leading me by the nose, and forgetting my benefactions, and thus it is no more proper to believe you than dogs; whereas, if it had not been for me and my care for you, and the love which I showed you, knaves that you are, never would it have come to your eventual release from this grievous gaol. And, therefore, I swear

by the most holy prophet Mahomet, that, as I have been
your best friend, so, from this day forth, will I be your
most deadly enemy, and will seek out causes to hinder
you from ever coming out of this tower. Dogs! traitors!
perjurers! faithless Pagans! will you thus repay my
kindnesses, who have been to you as your own father?"

We acknowledged before all the Turks that it was
indeed so, and that he was not our aga, but our father,
and had been the principal cause of our liberation, and
had done us such kindnesses that we should never be
able to repay and recompense them to the day of our
death. Moreover, as it was impossible for us to make
arrangements for the money with the merchants, we
offered to subscribe with our own blood that we would
send him, by way of Venice, in half-a-year at latest, 500
ducats, and also handsome knives, and striking-clocks;
and this we promised to fulfil upon our soul and faith.
But he would not allow himself to be appeased by anything, but reviled and cursed us till the foam ran out of
his mouth; he also ordered us to be immediately put
into irons, and, uttering strange threats against us, commanded us to go into the tower.

When we came to our companions, and told them that
we could not negotiate the loan of the money anywhere,
there was great weeping and lamentation. And now
that we had angered the aga, who had been our very
good friend, and had no one any more to manage our
affairs, all hope departed that anything should come of
our liberation, and we returned, with a downcast heart,
to our trade of knitting gloves and stockings, and longed
every hour to die, and be once for all freed from these
miseries. And verily, even as we had been greatly en-

raptured from having had a sure hope of deliverance, even so, on the other hand, were we affected by great and boundless melancholy when all hope was taken from us, especially when the aga came to us in a fortnight and declared that we must not hope to quit the tower, because the Sultan, as well as Ibrahim Pasha and the Christian ambassadors, had gone from Constantinople, and that, whereas we could have procured our freedom for 200 ducats, we had purposely deprived ourselves of it. He also caused us to be told several times by the guards that we must remain in the tower till the Sultan returned from the war. At this we were exceedingly terrified, and, fully believing that it was so, wept heartily over our misery and misfortune; nevertheless, we ceased not to implore the aga, for the sake of the recompence of their prophet Mahomet, to allow us to go only once more among the merchants and try to borrow the money. But he would not give permission, but declared that it was too late, and all our negotiating was in vain.

Here every man can estimate how we poor prisoners felt about the heart when, after having had a fortnight ago a certain hope of liberation, that hope was unexpectedly taken from us; and verily it was with us just as with a man who has climbed out of a deep well up to the wall that surmounts it, when, just as he is about to step out, his hands have given way, and he has fallen back again into the deep well, without having any hope of climbing out of it any more. While I write this, and call that time to remembrance, I feel even now how mournful my heart was then, and cannot write more upon that subject for sorrow. Therefore, praised for ever and ever be the Lord God Most High, whom, out of His

boundless mercy, it pleased to deliver me from that excess
of misery and bitterness of heart, yea, from that grievous
prison, and to restore me happily to my dear fatherland.

When we had bewept ourselves to our heart's content, had given up all hope, and had returned again to
our trade, then, unexpectedly, did the Lord Most High
look upon our misery, and of His holy graciousness it
pleased Him to assist us, so that a Spanish merchant,
named Alfonzo di Strada, who had earned his freedom
from a Turkish prison by work and service, and had
married and settled in the city of Galata, sent us word
by one of our guards, who used to take our gloves and
purses to that city to market and sell them, that letters
had arrived for us from Christendom, and advised us
once more, that is to say, Zahradetzky, the priest John,
and myself, to beg leave of absence from the aga, and
to entertain hopes of making arrangements for the
money.   Doubting whether he would let us go, and
especially knowing, according to the aga's information,
that it was already too late, we were not much delighted
at this message; nevertheless, since it must be so, we
allowed ourselves to entreat him to let us go, at any rate,
this once more to Galata.   But he replied that we were
only devising an excuse in order to be able to make an
excursion; that previously, when we had time and leave
to go about, we had not chosen to exert ourselves about
the money; and that now, when it was too late, and we
knew that it was too late, we were willing to exert ourselves in earnest.   With this answer he left us in sorrow.
Nevertheless, in the morning he ordered us three to be
summoned out of the tower, asked us whether we intended to trouble ourselves about the money in earnest,

and promised that he would kindly forgive us all the
anger we had caused him by deluding him so long.

On hearing this we kissed his hand with tears, and
promised not to return without the money. And, list-
ening to our earnest desire, he sent with us four Turks
as guards, with whom we went to Galata, and to the
house of this Strada. When we asked him where we
could make arrangements about the money, according
to his message, he at first held back with gloomy reserve,
saying,—"I don't know; I certainly imagined that a certain good friend of yours intended to advance it for you,
but to-day he says he has none." At this we were un-
speakably downcast. Seeing us thus downcast, he could
not restrain himself from weeping, but delivered us letters from the priest Adam von Winor, Dean of Carl-
stein, and from my dear mother, the noble Lady Cathe-
rine Wratislaw, _née_ Von Bessin, wherein they informed
us that they had sent us three 200 ducats by way of
Venice, which Alfonzo di Strada was to pay us. When,
therefore, we asked for the money, and he showed it
us, so unlooked-for and inexpressibly sudden a joy filled
our hearts that it is in no wise possible to describe it.
We immediately embraced and kissed Strada with tears
of joy, and not even waiting for the food and drink
which he wished to give us, as a bird which escapes
from its cage, settles somewhere on a tree, sings and
delights in its liberty, even so we, being enraptured
beyond all our expectations, praised the Lord God, returned to our tower with the money, and hastened up
into the fortress with a cheerful countenance.

Our aga, seeing us somewhat cheerful, contrary to our
previous mood, immediately understood that we had the

money, and asked us how it was that we had been successful? We kissed his hand, and threw the 200 ducats, purse
and all, into his lap, and besought him that we might not
go into the prison anymore, but that our companions also
might be liberated. He counted over the ducats and received them with thanks, and patting us on the head, commended us for having done well, and paid him the money
according to promise. He then said that he forgave us
all, and commanded us that day to be all released from our
irons, and to be set free the next day and conducted to the
English embassy at Galata. In fact, we were released
—and that immediately—by the gipsy smiths, from our
irons and fetters, and could not sleep all night long for
joy, but tied our rags together, distributed something to
the poor prisoners who remained there after us, and bade
adieu to them; for the poor fellows wept bitterly, knowing that they were to remain still longer in that miserable prison, and must almost despair of their freedom.
These prisoners were,—Balak Dak Istwan, a lieutenant
from Erlau, who had already been fourteen years in the
tower, Matthias, the hussar, and Christopher, the innkeeper, all three Hungarians; the fourth was the German
from Hernstein, who had been a lieutenant in the Croatian
fortress Wysyne. These miserable prisoners begged
us, if we reached Christendom, to entreat our Emperor
on their behalf, that they might be freed from that cruel
tower by the exchange of other Turks for them. This
we promised to do.

Next day we bade adieu to them with great weeping,
and quitted, on the festival of St. Peter and St. Paul,
that most gloomy Black Tower, in which we had been
shut up two years and five weeks without intermission,

and going to the aga, thanked him and the rest of the
guards for the kindness and favour they had shown us,
and promised (and also afterwards fulfilled our promise)
to send them handsome knives, and the aga a striking-
clock. The aga then had us conducted to the English
ambassador at Galata, who received us in a friendly
manner, and ordered a bath to be prepared for us, that
we might be cleansed from the filthy condition in which
we were. After the bath we visited the Catholic churches,
of which there are seven in Galata, and gave thanks
to the Lord God for our deliverance from so exceeding
cruel an imprisonment, fervently beseeching Him to
be our Guide and Gracious Protector to our own dear
country.

About that time Sultan Mehemet marched with great
pomp from Constantinople, with all his court and his
principal warriors, and having had tents pitched before
the city, rested there several days according to custom,
waiting for more soldiers. For several pashas from Egypt,
Palestine, Cairo, and other lands beyond sea, were still
marching up with their armies, and they were waiting
for them. Verily, we might gaze and wonder at the
beautiful order which the Turks kept while pitching the
tents, the camp being so extensive that no one could
see to the end of it. Mehemet Pasha marched an hour
before midnight with 50,000 men, always keeping a day's
journey before the Emperor and the main army, and had
the roads put in order, and tents pitched for the Sultan
and the principal officers of the army, so that all the
tents were changed and pitched before the Sultan came
up, and stood in readiness, measured out into streets
foursquare, like a fortress, with bastions and trenches.

O

In the centre of the whole camp were placed large iron
tents for the Emperor, his chamberlains and courtiers,
and also for his horses and carriages, and the pashas and
their attendants, and that in such numbers that one
might lose one's way among them, just as in a large city.
There were also gates made of waxed linen, and so beset
by the Emperor's guard that no one could get to the
Sultan's tent without permission.

When Mehemet Pasha moved forward from the camp,
to secure the safety of the road, and marched with his
50,000 men, there was no clamour, noise, or trumpeting
to be heard, only small drums were beaten, and that
sparingly, merely that the soldiers might know how to
direct themselves. And when they wanted to stop for
the night, they pitched their tents without any tumult,
and struck them again in the morning, and placed them
on camels and mules, so quietly, that it was a wonder
to behold; and truth it is that with us fifty soldiers
make more disorder and shouting than these 50,000 made.
After Mehemet Pasha marched the Emperor and his
main army, he himself riding in the centre of them with
his usual guard of janissaries, spahis, and other soldiers,
and with chief pashas in great numbers. On the right
rode always 12,000 spahis and oglungars with yellow
plumes on their lances ; on the left, the same number of
horse-soldiers with red flags on their lances, like a field
of poppies in bloom ; in front of the Emperor himself
marched 12,000 janissaries on foot; next rode the Sultan
and the pashas, and after him the sangiaks of all his
lands.   While marching through the open country, they
beat large drums without intermission.   Behind the
Sultan rode all his courtiers, and last of all Cykula Pasha,

with the renegades, or Christians, who had become Mahometans, and other Turks, he having about 15,000 people
under him. Round the Emperor himself were solaks
and kapigis, with bows and arrows, and also chamberlains, who corrected anything that was wrong, and took
care that the march should be conducted in good order,
and managed all manner of amusements for the Emperor
on the road. They had wonderful jugglers amongst them,
who wrestled, leapt, and swung before the Sultan; some
of whom stood on the saddle with their feet even, when
their horses were galloping, turned somersaults, leapt
into the saddle and down again at full gallop, and exhibited many more amusing tricks.

When the Sultan had marched from Constantinople
with the main army, the beglerbeg of the land of Greece
pitched his tent with the rest of the army, about 80,000
strong, in the same place where the Emperor had previously been, and rested there two days. The English
ambassador stayed with us two days at Galata, and on
the third day we marched in good order with these 80,000,
always pitching our tents where the Emperor had rested
for the night. When we arrived at Greek Belgrade, the
whole army was concentrated together, amounting, as
they said, to 500,000 men, but there were not really so
many. There might have been full 300,000 of all sorts,
including the rabble and worthless mob, the muleteers,
and drivers of asses and camels. By that city they pitched
their camp, extending so far that it was impossible to
see to the end of it. The Emperor would not lodge in
the castle, but lay in the open country; and some thousand Tatars also joined him, who day and night were
burning the villages of Christians living under the pro-

tection of the Turks, and driving herds of cattle, and droves of unbroken mares into the camp. These Tatars obtained such an abundance of cattle that they sold two Hungarian oxen for a dollar, more or less, and cows for twenty or thirty aspers the pair. We, too, bought a calf from under a cow for eight aspers, and eat meat to our heart's content. The Turks, on killing an ox, cut the flesh into long thin stripes, salted it, stretched ropes from one tent to another, hung the meat on them and dried it in the sun. At that time, too, the Tatars captured many Christians daily and brought them to the Sultan. The Sultan lay before Belgrade for about a fortnight.

Meanwhile the English ambassador made application to Ibrahim Pasha to send us to Buda and set us at liberty, because he wished to write to our Emperor about making peace. He also procured us access to him and the aga in command of the janissaries, and when we were admitted into his presence in his tent, we kissed his feet, and besought him to set us free before the mighty Sultan marched to Erlau, because, eventually, our Emperor, owing to us, would send off commissioners to humble themselves to the Sultan in his stead, and sue for peace. The pasha asked us whether we had seen all their camp, the great might, and the number of the countless multitude of people that was marching against the giaours? When we replied that we had not seen it and could not see it, since we had travelled in the rearmost body amongst the camels and mules, he immediately commanded us to be conducted throughout the whole camp, and to be shown the artillery and other engines of war. When we had seen everything that we could that day, we were again summoned in the morning before the same pasha, with the English ambassador, and asked whether we had now seen the exceeding great power and might of their Emperor? And whether our king could collect as many men and stand in array against them? We gave for answer that we had seen all, and never in our lives had we seen so many soldiers, and that it was not possible for our Emperor to collect such a number of men ; and surely our Emperor knew nothing about the Sultan's great forces, otherwise he would immediately treat for peace, would humble himself to the Turkish emperor, and would certainly send presents to appease the anger of so mighty a lord. Therefore, we besought him to set us free the sooner, that we might make that exceeding mighty force known to our Emperor and all the Christians. And he replied that he would do so, but that we were to remember the kindnesses shown us, noise their great forces abroad everywhere, and induce the Christians to make peace before they arrived at Erlau. And if our Emperor wished to send any of us to the Turkish emperor to negotiate such a peace, we were not to fear aught, but boldly and willingly to make ourselves useful in the matter, he swearing by the beard of the Sultan, his lord, that no harm should happen to us, but that we should be presented with distinguished gifts, handsome clothes and horses, and dismissed in safety to our own country.

When we had promised all this and much more, a letter credential and emancipatory was given us, and also one to the pasha at Buda, (five of our party having been in a tower there ever since the death of my lord the resident,) to the effect that he was to release them from prison, and entrust us to boatmen, to go to a fortress of our own up the Danube. In return for this kindness we all fell at his feet and thanked him. It was our great good fortune, that we received the letter to the pasha at Buda, and the letter credential that day, for, had it not happened so, we should certainly have all been cut in pieces, as will soon be related.

When the Turkish emperor moved from this place with his whole army, and began to march towards Erlau, they formed, in a very beautiful plain, opposing armies of camels, mules, and horses, amounting to full 150,000 in number, and so extensive that it was impossible to see to the end of them; they drew up as though they were about to engage in battle, fired cannons and all their heavy artillery at each other, surrounded the body which represented the Christians, skirmished, turned it to flight, took many thousands prisoners, and flattered their Emperor, giving him good hopes of victory, and continuing to advance quietly, and in good order, further and further into the land of Hungary.

When we arrived at the fortress of Zolnak we heard news that our people had taken the fortress of Hatwan from the Turks, that the Walloons had behaved like dogs, and not like Christians to the Turks, their wives, and children, had ripped up pregnant women, had cut children at the breast in two, had hung their mothers up by the breasts, had flayed and embowelled them, had searched for money, and had so tortured them, that it was grievous to hear the lamentations of the Turks, who affirmed that it was not the Walloons, but the Germans who had exercised such cruelty. Hence arose among the Turks not only the beforementioned clamour, weeping, and lamentation, but also acts of ferocious cruelty. For whatever lately-captured prisoners they had they cut in pieces, and bound themselves by a great oath, that, if they took any fortress of ours, they would behave therein in a similar way in return, and would not spare and leave alive any German, either woman, old man, or child, nay, not even a dog that belonged to a German. In this ill-humour they wished to sabre even the Christian ambassadors, and more especially us prisoners, and would have carried this into execution had it not been, firstly, for the Divine protection, and secondly, for Ibrahim Pasha and the aga in command of the janissaries, who immediately surrounded the whole place where the Christian ambassadors were living with us with a strong guard of janissaries, and allowed no one to have access to us. Orders were then given to us not to show ourselves to any one, but to remain in our tent, and not to quit it under pain of death.

As the Turks remained three days at Zolnak for sorrow and never moved, our ambassador kept constantly applying to the pasha, through his chiaous, that, according to his promise, fifty hussars, or Turkish archers, should be assigned us, to escort us as far as Buda. But the pasha was vehemently enraged, and threatened to have us all put to the sword, asking whether it was in return for this that he was to set us at liberty, because our fathers, uncles, and brothers, had behaved so dishonourably to their dear friends the Turks at Hatwan? Although, if they had murdered the men only, it would have been no wonder, since the nature of war often brings that with it ; but it was a doggish, brutal, and unheard-of thing to behave thus cruelly to the innocent female sex and little chil-

dren; and, if he had not appeased the anger of the Sultan
and chief officials, we should have long ago been cut in
pieces. Therefore, he bade him leave him quiet in the
matter, and not press him, if he did not wish to meet
with something worse himself.

When the English ambassador sorrowfully made
known this sad intelligence to us, and said that we were
in danger of our lives, we were greatly terrified and
cast down. He also counselled us to pray fervently to
the Lord God, that, since it had pleased him to free us
from so grievous a prison, it might please Him to be our
God still further, and grant us a happy return to our
own dear country. And as he understood, that, as soon
as the camp moved, we might have some difficulty, and
might even perhaps be put to the sword, he cared for us
faithfully, hired four peasant carts to go to Buda, gave
us 100 ducats for the journey, assigned us his own interpreter, and a janissary to guard us, and counselled us
in God's name, as soon as the Emperor marched towards
Erlau, to turn by another way towards Buda, and commit
ourselves to the Lord God, since we already had our
credentials and the letter to the Pasha of Buda.

As we were obliged to travel that night by a most
dangerous road, where day and night the Turks and
Tatars and our hussars were skirmishing—and, in fact,
they brought into the camp daily captured heyduks of
ours, and wounded hussars, and also multitudes of
Christians' heads—we were constrained to swear to the
janissary that, if Christians came upon us, no harm
should happen to him, and he, on his part, promised in
return that, if Turks came upon us, we should travel
on in safety, since we had the Turkish emperor's pass-

port; but he acknowledged that he could not make any promise for the Tatars if we fell into their hands, but said that he should be cut in pieces with us himself, for the Tatars did not even spare a Turk, but when they fall upon them by tens or twenties, and are more than a match for them, they sabre them, and plunder them of everything, without paying the least regard to any orders. For this reason we took a guide with us, and, after bidding adieu to the ambassador of the English queen, and thanking him for his great kindness, as soon as the Sultan moved from Zolnak towards Erlau we turned, with great terror, towards Buda, in the name of God.

As we went on our way we kept continually looking back, with a timid and terrified heart, to see whether they were pursuing us, and were in constant expectation of being cut to pieces, since we were obliged to travel through the most dangerous localities, where Turks, Tatars, and Christians were skirmishing, it being impossible, as our guide informed us, to go by any other road. Nevertheless, it pleased a merciful God so to order it that during the whole day, from morning dawn to evening twilight, we never met a single human being; only on arriving, when it was almost twilight, at a large Hungarian village, we saw about a hundred Tatars moving about the vineyards. Filled with terror, we hastened to the village, which was entirely surrounded by a moat, and besought the inhabitants to protect us against the Tatars and admit us into the village, which they did. The poor peasants threw a little bridge over the moat, bade us sorrowfully welcome, and informed us what excessive ill-treatment they were compelled to endure from the Tatars, about 500 of whom were encamped in the village. They, therefore, counselled us to go without delay to the vicarage, and conceal ourselves somewhere, that the Tatars might not see us. We listened to their advice, went to the vicar, and begged him to open the church to us. He kindly gave us cheese and slices of bread, and admitted us into the church, where, with a contrite heart, we besought God for mercy and protection against the Tatars. Not knowing what plan to adopt, we also hoped in the janissary, and trusted that our Turkish passport would be available for us. But the janissary was as much afraid of the Tatars as ourselves, and consequently turned quite pale, and forbad us to speak to him in Turkish.

Meanwhile the Tatars lighted large fires in the village, roasted oxen and sheep whole, cut off the cooked flesh, and ate like dogs. When we quitted the church, and began to feed our horses, the Tatars got intelligence of us, and immediately crowded to us, to the number of about 200, and, surrounding us, asked us who and what we were. We and the janissary made them a low Turkish obeisance, answered that we were going to Buda by order of the Sultan, and exhibited the Sultan's letters. But they replied, contemptuously, that it would be an improper thing to let us go, and sent for their captain, and the good God knows what they intended to do with us. Perceiving that it would not go well with us, and that we should either be made prisoners, or put to the sword by them, we prayed very penitently in heart, and besought God that it might please Him to be our protector, which, in fact, came to pass at sunset.

Wonder of wonders, and mighty power of God! Although the whole of that day had been very bright, the sun shining beautifully throughout, and not the least vapour or cloud had been visible, it nevertheless pleased a most merciful God, who never forsaketh them that trust in Him, to raise an exceedingly violent wind, and after it a tempest, so that it did not rain but pour, and a water-spout must have burst. The whole village and the trenches were filled with water, and the Tatars returned to their horses, the tempest having extinguished all their fires. During this violent tempest we harnessed our horses to the carriages, by the advice of the poor peasants, and quitted the village, taking with us a peasant to guide us by a route different from that which we had intended to pursue, as there were Tatars encamped in all the surrounding villages. This violent rain lasted without intermission till midnight, and during it we nevertheless travelled onwards, though we were obliged to pull the horses and carriages out of quagmires and help them forwards. We also travelled through a great number of burnt and forsaken villages, and heard the crying, weeping, and wailing of the poor people, and the lowing of the captured cattle. However, we made our way gradually onwards, for God strengthened our horses and ourselves, and arrived, about three hours before daybreak, at a heath, where we gave our horses hay and rested ourselves. But as soon as the horses had eaten a little we recommenced our journey. Our guides, owing to the rain, wandered far from the road, and could not remember whither they had led us; they were also anxious to escape from us. The janissary, perceiving this, did not allow them to leave him for a moment, but tied them both by the neck with a strap, and drove them

before him to show him the way, threatening to cut off
their heads if they did not conduct us to a good road.
Terrified at this, they groped for the road with their
hands, but continually led us further and further from
the right way.

When day was about to dawn, our guides terrified us
exceedingly by being utterly unable to remember where
they were, and by saying that they heard the stamping
of horses and shouting of men, and were, therefore,
afraid of falling into the hands of the Tatars, who were
encamped in all directions round about. They advised
us to lie down with one ear to the ground and listen ;
we should find that the ground shook, and, in short, that
a number of men, how many they could not say, were
riding towards us. This we did with infinite terror,
and ascertained that the ground really did shake, and
that the noise of men and neighing of horses were to be
heard. We therefore halted, and deliberated what was
to be done. When it grew more light we espied a grove
of no great size in a wide plain, and, not being able to distinguish what it was, declared unanimously that it was a
body of Tatars, and some of us affirmed that they saw a
banner waving. Not knowing how else to help ourselves,
we all made up our minds to disperse, and each seek for
safety where he best could. However, one of our drivers
crept on all-fours towards the grove, wishing to know
what in the world it was, and, on creeping nearer to it,
saw that it was only a grove, cried out " Jesus," and
told us not to be afraid. Then the poor dear janissary
imagined that it was Christians, and wanted to take to
flight, but some of us held his horse under him, and
prevented him from escaping. At length, just as if

we had awoke from sleep, we approached the grove, and jeered each other about the panic which that little bit of a wood had struck into us. Passing beyond the grove, and it beginning now to be daylight, we espied about thirty Turkish hussars, with lances and pennons, galloping straight towards us, who placed their lances in the rest, shouted, "*Allah! Allah!*" surrounded us, and placed the points of their lances against our breasts. At this we were greatly terrified, but our janissary recovered his self-possession as soon as he heard them shout, and saluted them in Turkish. They asked us who and whence we were, and whither we were going, and, on receiving an answer from the janissary, cried out, "*Jury pre jury!*" spurred their horses and darted away from us. These Turks were from the division of the Pasha of Bosnia, who had sent them forwards to ascertain where the Sultan was, and when he intended to march to Erlau. Then, at length, our guides remembered where they were, and conducted us in an oblique direction into the right road, which leads to Pesth.

When day had fully dawned we heard loud salvos of artillery from Buda, which, at so great a distance, was surprising to us. It again occurred that no one met us on our journey till it was just noon, when we saw a large number of cavalry riding towards us on the plain. When they approached us we found that it was an exceedingly fine body of about 10,000 cavalry, with which the Pasha of Bosnia was on his way to reinforce the Sultan at Erlau. They all had long lances and various-coloured pennons upon them. As soon as they espied us about a hundred of them darted forwards, and rode at full gallop towards us with their lances in the rest.

As soon as our janissary knew that they were Turks, he dismounted, saluted them, and informed them who we were and whither he was conducting us. Our interpreter also rode with him to the pasha, showed him our letters, and informed him that the Sultan was already moving towards Erlau with his whole army. He then returned to us again. When the pasha's army had passed us, we made for Pesth, and arrived at the city about an hour before sunset.* Our janissary showed our letters to the cadi, and requested him to assign us a lodging, which was done. Although we were now safe from the Tatars, we were, nevertheless, still afraid that the Turks might send for us back, and order us to be again detained in prison.

In the morning, when the pasha returned home, the Sultan's letter was delivered to him by us, in which orders were given him to escort us to the nearest Christian fortress, and set at liberty our five comrades, who had been in prison at Buda ever since the death of our ambassador. The pasha read the letter through, and not only immediately set our comrades at liberty, but also gave us plenty to eat and drink, and ordered boatmen†

---

* Literally, *the twenty-third hour.* This is the old Bohemian and Polish reckoning from sunset to sunset. There is still a twenty-four-hour clock outside the *Rathshaus* in the *Altstadt* at Prague.

† *Martalozes.* This word appears to mean "*boatmen,*" and is possibly connected with the French " matelot;" but it is omitted in Sumawsky's dictionary, and Jungmann merely conjectures its meaning, and quotes this passage. The more usual meaning would be *kidnappers,* which is quite inapplicable here. It may, however, well mean the boatmen, &c. usually employed on predatory excursions up the Danube for the purpose of taking prisoners to sell as slaves.

to take us up stream to the fortress of Towaschow. At this we were the more delighted in proportion to the greatness of the doubts we had previously entertained about being so easily allowed to go up the Danube; for, remembering the Turks' wrath and fury on account of the taking of Hatwan, we were every hour in expectation that they would send after us, with orders for our arrest and imprisonment. But it pleased a merciful God to preserve us from this fate.

The next day, early in the morning, we sent the peasants, with the carriages and some of our things, forwards to Towaschow, requesting them to inform the Christian soldiers there of our liberation and arrival, and intending to recompense them there for the use of the carriages. But the poor fellows fell in with some Tatars and were put to the sword by them. We then got into a boat, and were pulled up stream, while our janissary and dragoman, or interpreter, rode on horseback along the bank. When we got close to Towaschow, we saw the bastions full of German soldiers, and imagined that our peasants had already made known our approach in the fortress. Such, however, was not the case. For a few days before some Turks, disguised in women's clothes, had sailed in a boat to the very skirts of the fortress, had seized and bound two fishermen and a woman, and had carried them off to Buda. Thus the people at Towaschow imagined that some more Turks were coming on a plundering expedition, and had disguised themselves like captives, in order the more easily to delude the Christians. Moreover, seeing the janissary and dragoman on the other bank of the Danube, they determined to allow us to approach the fortress within point-blank range of their cannon. Being then so close to the fortress, and not knowing what to do for joy, we began to embrace and kiss each other. At this moment our friends fired two pieces, one at the janissary, and the other at our boat, so that the water splashed over us, the artilleryman having fired a little too low. The boatmen, therefore, saw their danger, and wanted to let us fall again down stream. We prevented them from doing this, took the oars out of their hands, and raising a hat on the point of a spear, called out with a loud voice that we were Christians. The commander, Rosenhahn, a German by birth, saw this, and stepping up to the artilleryman, forbad him to fire any more, otherwise he would have shot our boat through with a second discharge, and we must have been drowned. In fact, I afterwards ascertained myself that he had taken better aim than the first time, and would certainly not have missed us.

Terrified as we were, we, nevertheless, approached the fortress, and calling out in German and Hungarian, made known who we were. Then there came to meet us a couple of boats, with two guns each, which first made a circuit round us, that we might not escape, and occupied the Danube behind us. They then rowed straight up to us, with their firearms cocked, and asked who we were. Upon our briefly informing them, they immediately lashed our boat to theirs, and pulled to the front of the fortress, where we got out, and all kneeling down, thanked God with heartfelt tears for our deliverance from so grievous an imprisonment. We were conducted into the fortress, cordially welcomed by the governor, and well-supplied with meat and drink. We informed him that the janissary, who had been our escort, was on the other side with a dragoman, and requested that they might be sent for, as they had letters to deliver to the governor.   This was done, and they were entertained in the town, where we, too, remained for the night.

In the morning we went in a boat to Gran, and saw sick and dead soldiers lying everywhere on the bank of the Danube.   They stretched out their hands to us,—some of them being half dead,—and besought us, for God's sake, to take them to Gran.   In fact we did take three, but two of them died on the way, and the third we conveyed to the camp.   When we disembarked in the night, in the neighbourhood of Gran, we came to a picquet of the regiment of Swabia, and, after declaring who and whence we were, were compelled to wait several hours on the spot, till the officer of the watch came to us with soldiers and torches, welcomed us, and took us into the camp.   In the morning, Maximilian, archduke of Austria, was pleased to send for us to come to him in the castle, where he questioned us about various matters, especially about the Sultan, inquiring whether he was marching to Erlau in person.   About this the archduke knew nothing whatever, and we were very much surprised that the Christians possessed such poor intelligence.   After relating him everything in a fitting manner, we gave him correct information about the strength of the Turkish forces, at which his grace was much surprised, and was greatly vexed at having been so erroneously informed.   He, therefore, immediately gave orders to sound an alarm, intending to march straight to Erlau.   But our people marched without at-

P

taining their object, and, failing to relieve Erlau, were obliged to leave that famous fortress in the hands of the Turks.

At Gran I met my cousin, Felix Wratislaw, and also Albert Wratislaw, who had been shot in the knee at Hatwan.   He afterwards died, and lies buried at Gran. We then begged his grace the archduke to have us conveyed to Vienna, for our feet were blistered, and we could not walk well from exhaustion.   He granted our request, and ordered us to be conveyed to Vienna.

We arrived at Vienna, which was then under his grace the Archduke Maximilian, and were permitted to have an audience. We kissed his hand, and after giving him certain information about the Sultan's march, and the strength of his army, petitioned for pecuniary assistance to enable us to travel to Prague.   We obtained our request, and he not only gave us money for the journey, but also ordered us to be conveyed to Prague to his brother, his Imperial Majesty Rudolph the Second.

When we arrived at Prague, and met our friends, O! it is impossible to describe the joy!   His Majesty the Emperor, hearing of us, was graciously pleased to summon us to his presence.   We kissed his hand and related how much we had had to endure in his service for all Christendom, and humbly entreated him to be our gracious emperor, king, and lord, and to be pleased to grant us some acceptable recompence for it.   His majesty looked kindly upon us all, and said, in German,—" *Wir wollen thun!*" "We will do so!"   It was then his pleasure to leave us; and, although orders were certainly given by him that a considerable sum of money should be divided amongst us, yet God knows in whose hands it remained; for 100, and 150 dollars, more or less, were given to some of us, who were foreigners, to enable them to reach their homes; whereas, after much entreaty, and many applications, nothing was given to us Bohemians, but merely the offer made that, if we liked to take service in the Emperor's court, we should take precedence of others. But we committed all to God, and preferred to return without money to our parents, friends, and acquaintances, who received us, as everybody can judge, with exceeding joy of heart. Thus, every one of us may, and ought to rejoice at this, and thank God, the best of comforters and succourers in sorrow, with heart and lips, to the day of his death. For, when all hope failed, all succour came to nought, and it seemed impossible to all men, both Turks and Christians, that we should return to our own country out of a prison so grievous, and, in all human judgment, so beyond the possibility of liberation, He set us at liberty by His mighty hand, to Whom, One true and living GOD in Trinity, be ascribed honour, glory, and praise for ever and ever!

CHISWICK PRESS:—PRINTED BY WHITTINGHAM AND WILKINS, TOOKS COURT, CHANCERY LANE.

For EU product safety concerns, contact us at Calle de José Abascal, 56–1°,
28003 Madrid, Spain or eugpsr@cambridge.org.